Libro de actividades y cuentos

Lada Josefa Kratky

ACKNOWLEDGMENTS

Grateful acknowledgment is given for the use of the following illustrations:
Winifred Barnum-Newman: 5, 11, 17, 23, 29, 35, 41, 47, 53, 59, 61, 65, 71, 77, 83, 89, 95, 101, 107, 113, 119, 125; Lada Josefa Kratky: 57, 58; Jane McCreary: 3, 4, 9, 10, 15, 16, 21, 22, 27, 28, 39, 40, 45, 46, 51, 52, 63, 64, 69, 70, 75, 76, 81, 82, 87, 88, 93, 94, 99, 100, 105, 106, 111, 112, 117, 118, 123, 124; Sharron O'Neil: 7, 8, 31, 32, 55, 56, 67, 68, 85, 86; John Sandford: 13, 14, 33, 34, 37, 38, 91, 92, 109, 110, 115, 116; Terri Starrett: 19, 20, 43, 44, 73, 74, 97, 98, 121, 122; Diana Thewlis: 25, 26, 49, 50, 79, 80, 103, 104, 127, 128.

Hampton-Brown Books
P.O. Box 223220
Carmel, California 93922
1-800-333-3510

Printed in the United States of America

ISBN 1-56334-580-3

09 10 11 12 13 14 33 32 31 30 29 28

O o oso

Eres cariñoso.

Escribe O o.

DIRECTIONS: Have children trace the *O-o*, identify the word that begins with *o* and circle the *o*. Then have them practice writing *o* in the box.

Querida familia:

Estamos estudiando la o. En el otro lado de esta hoja hay una rima sobre la o. Su hijo/a se la puede enseñar y pueden recitarla juntos.

En el siguiente cuadro, dibujen algunas cosas que empiecen con o, o peguen fotografías de esos objetos. Luego, completen la oración con el nombre de uno de ellos.

____________ empieza con o.

DIRECTIONS: Have children take this page home and work with their families to draw one or more objects whose names begin with *o*. Then, they complete the sentence with the name of one of them.

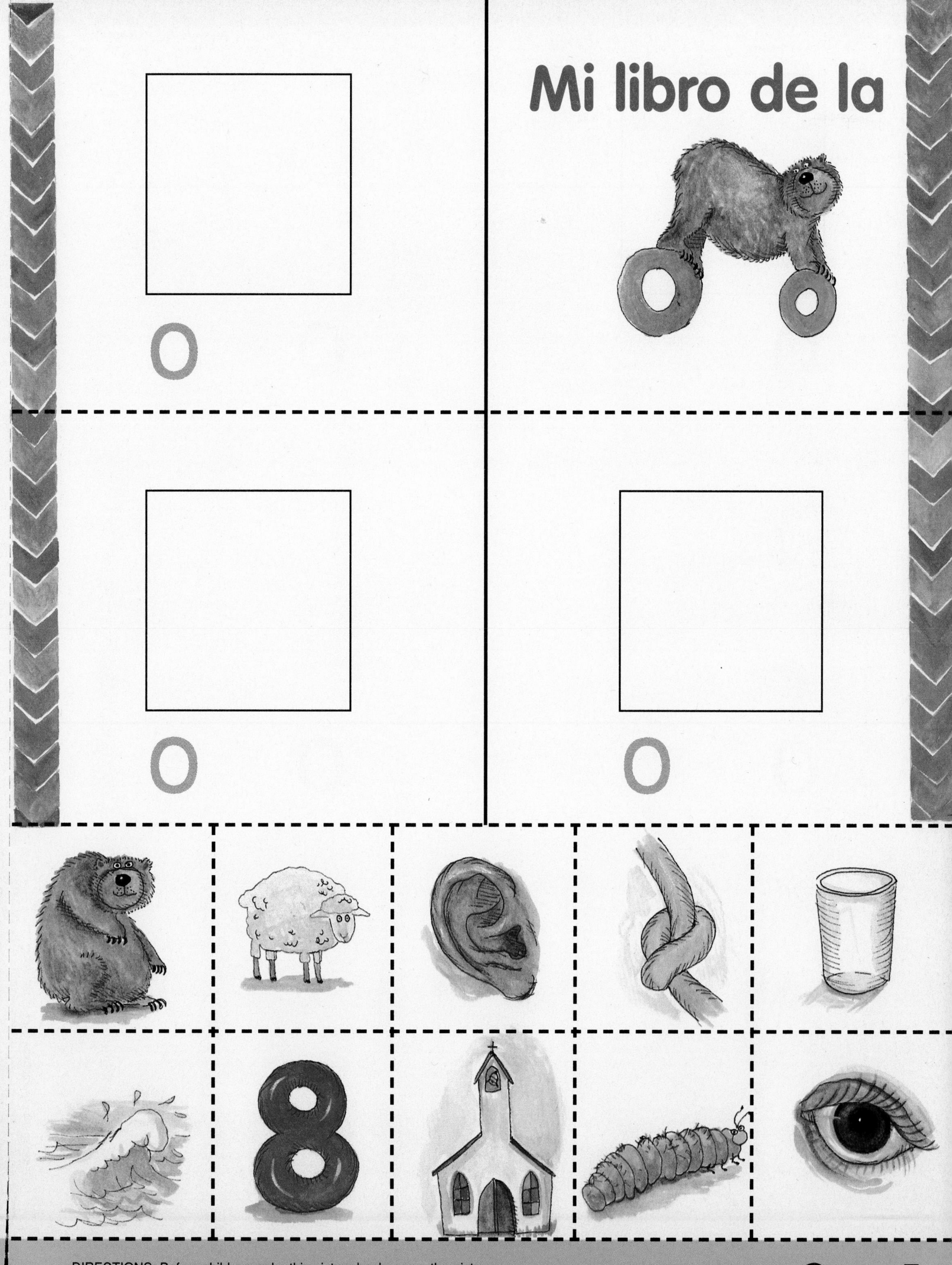

DIRECTIONS: Before children make this picture book, name the pictures: *oso, oveja, oreja, nudo, vaso, ola, ocho, iglesia, oruga, ojo.* Ask children to paste a picture whose name begins with *o* on each page and to trace the *o* as they say the name of the picture.

o
o
o
o

Osos

por ______________

oso azul

3

oso rojo

5

DIRECTIONS: Children make a six-page picture book. On each page, have them trace the *o* in *oso*. Read the book with children as they track the print.

oso
blanco

2

oso
verde

4

osos
amigos

6

A a araña

Mira su telaraña.

Escribe A a.

DIRECTIONS: Have children trace the *A-a*, identify the word that begins with *a* and circle the *a*. Then have them practice writing *a* in the box.

Querida familia:

Estamos estudiando la *a*. En el otro lado de esta hoja hay una rima sobre la *a*. Su hijo/a se la puede enseñar y pueden recitarla juntos.

En el siguiente cuadro, dibujen algunas cosas que empiecen con *a*, o peguen fotografías de esos objetos. Luego, completen la oración con el nombre de uno de ellos.

______________ empieza con a.

DIRECTIONS: Have children take this page home and work with their families to draw one or more objects whose names begin with *a*. Then, they complete the sentence with the name of one of them.

DIRECTIONS: Before children make this picture book, name the pictures: *araña, ballena, abeja, árbol, arco iris, jirafa, fotografía, anillo, avión, ardilla.* Ask children to paste a picture whose name begins with *a* on each page

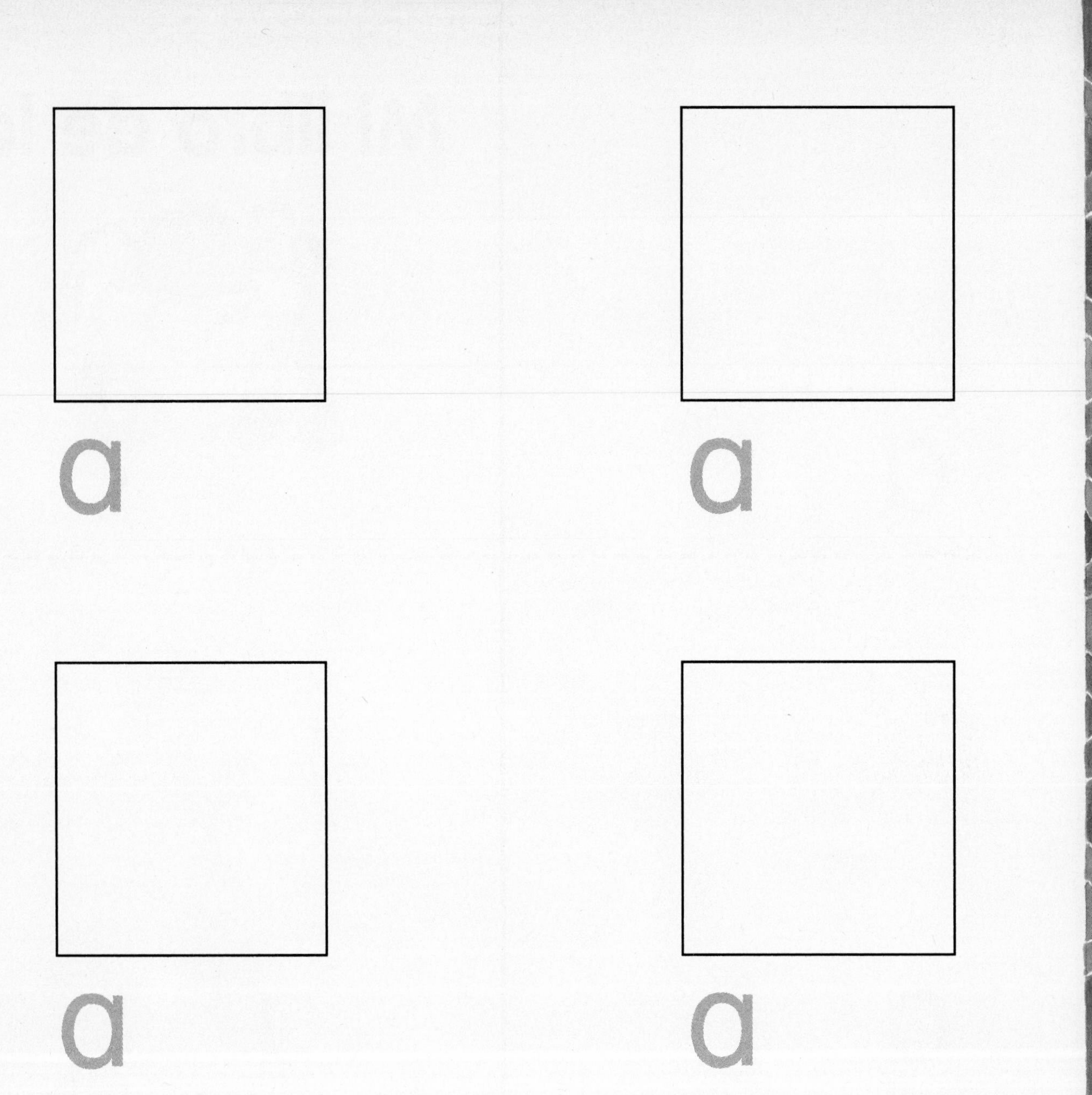
a
a
a
a

Fuera de aquí.

Arañas

por ____________

4 arañas

2 arañas

DIRECTIONS: Children make an eight-page picture book. On each page, have them trace the initial *a* in *araña*. Then read the book with children as they track the print.

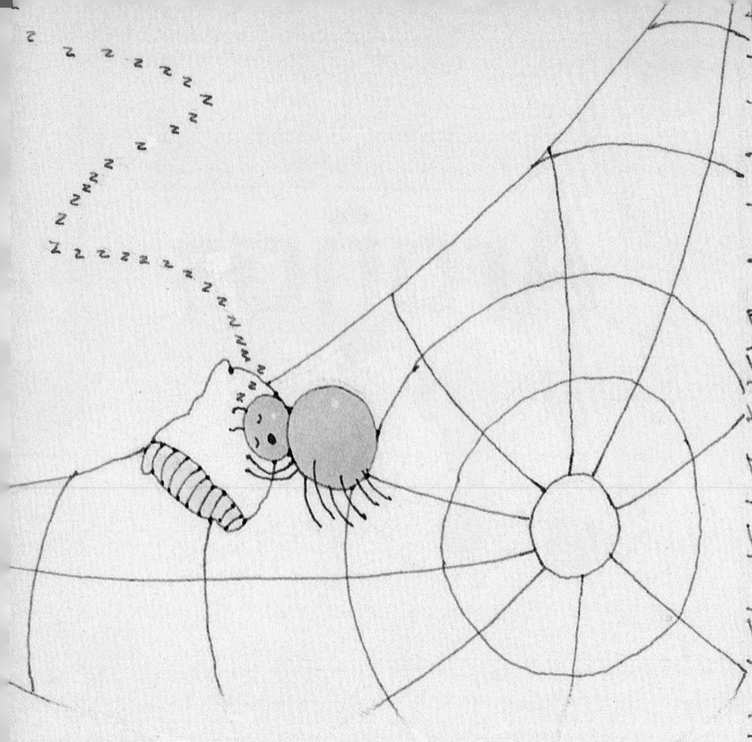

1 araña

5 arañas

3 arañas

¡Sí!

I i insecto

Se llama Héctor.

Escribe I i.

DIRECTIONS: Have children trace the *I-i*, identify the word that begins with *i* and circle the *i*. Then have them practice writing *i* in the box.

Querida familia:

Estamos estudiando la *i*. En el otro lado de esta hoja hay una rima sobre la *i*. Su hijo/a se la puede enseñar y pueden recitarla juntos.

En el siguiente cuadro, dibujen algunas cosas que empiecen con *i*, o peguen fotografías de esos objetos. Luego, completen la oración con el nombre de uno de ellos.

______________ empieza con i.

DIRECTIONS: Have children take this page home and work with their families to draw one or more objects whose names begin with *i*. Then, they complete the sentence with the name of one of them.

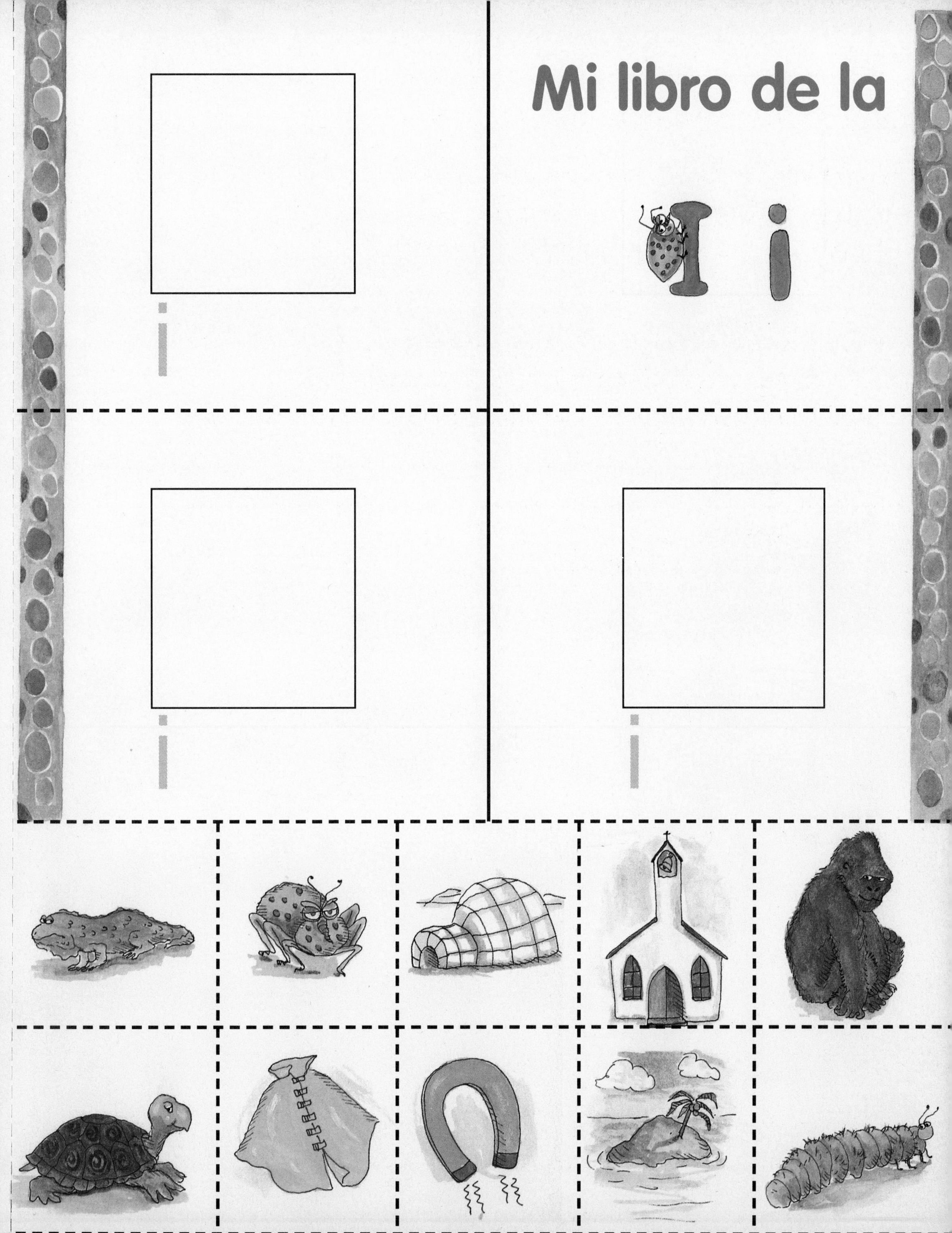

DIRECTIONS: Before children make this picture book, name the pictures: *iguana, insecto, iglú, iglesia, gorila, tortuga, impermeable, imán, isla, oruga*. Ask children to paste a picture whose name begins with *i* on each page and to trace the *i* as they say the name of the picture.

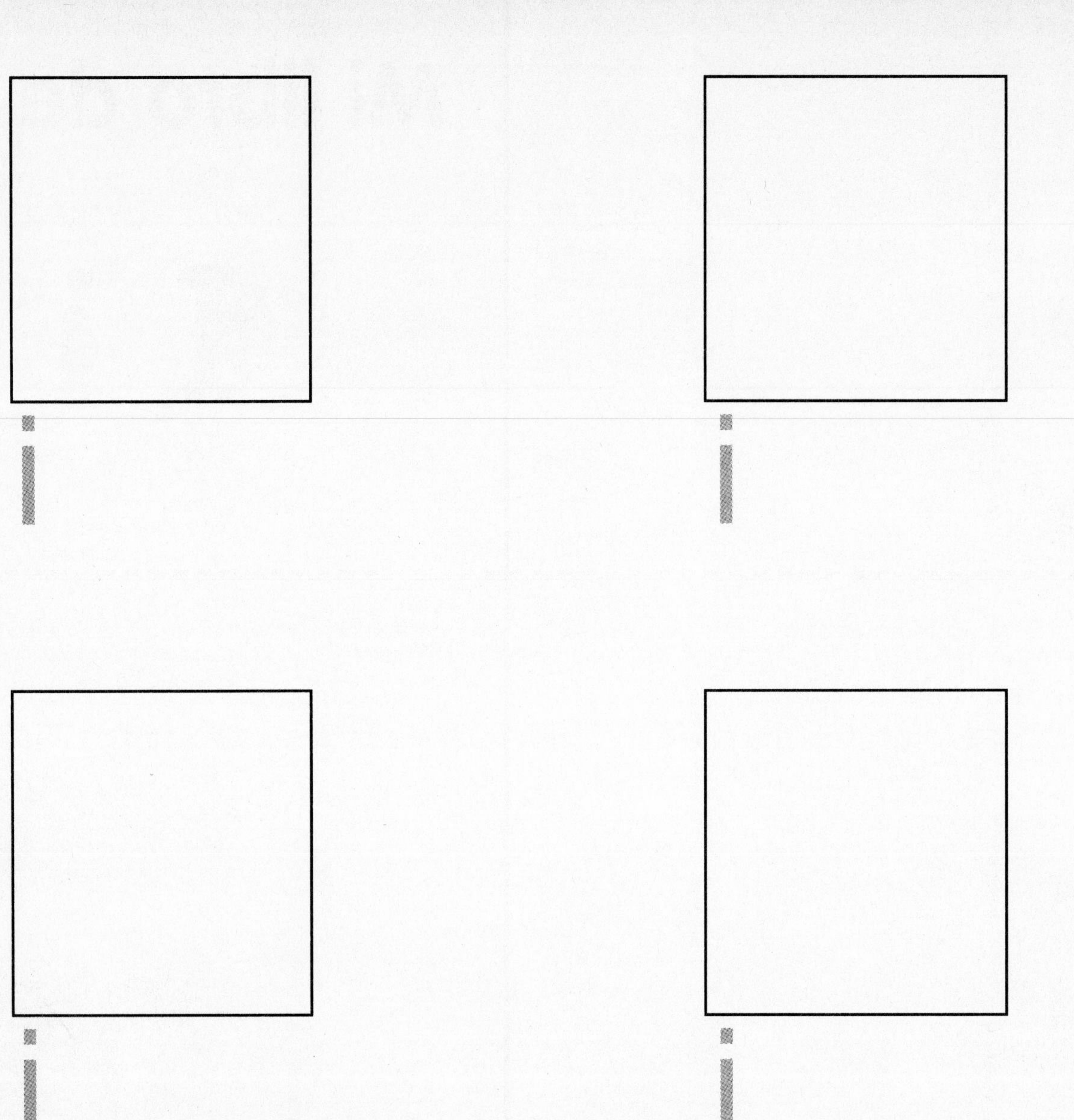

¡Cuántos insectos!

por ______________

insectos con puntos

3

insectos, insectos

5

DIRECTIONS: Children make a six-page picture book. Have them trace the initial *i* in words on each page. Then read the book with children as they track the print.

insectos a rayas

2

insectos en el jardín

4

insectos iguales, sin fin

6

E e elefante

Eres elegante.

Escribe E e.

DIRECTIONS: Have children trace the *E-e*, identify the word that begins with *e* and circle the *e*. Then have them practice writing *e* in the box.

Querida familia:

Estamos estudiando la *e*. En el otro lado de esta hoja hay una rima sobre la *e*. Su hijo/a se la puede enseñar y pueden recitarla juntos.

En el siguiente cuadro, dibujen algunas cosas que empiecen con *e*, o peguen fotografías de esos objetos. Luego, completen la oración con el nombre de uno de ellos.

______________ empieza con e.

DIRECTIONS: Have children take this page home and work with their families to draw one or more objects whose names begin with *e*. Then, they complete the sentence with the name of one of them.

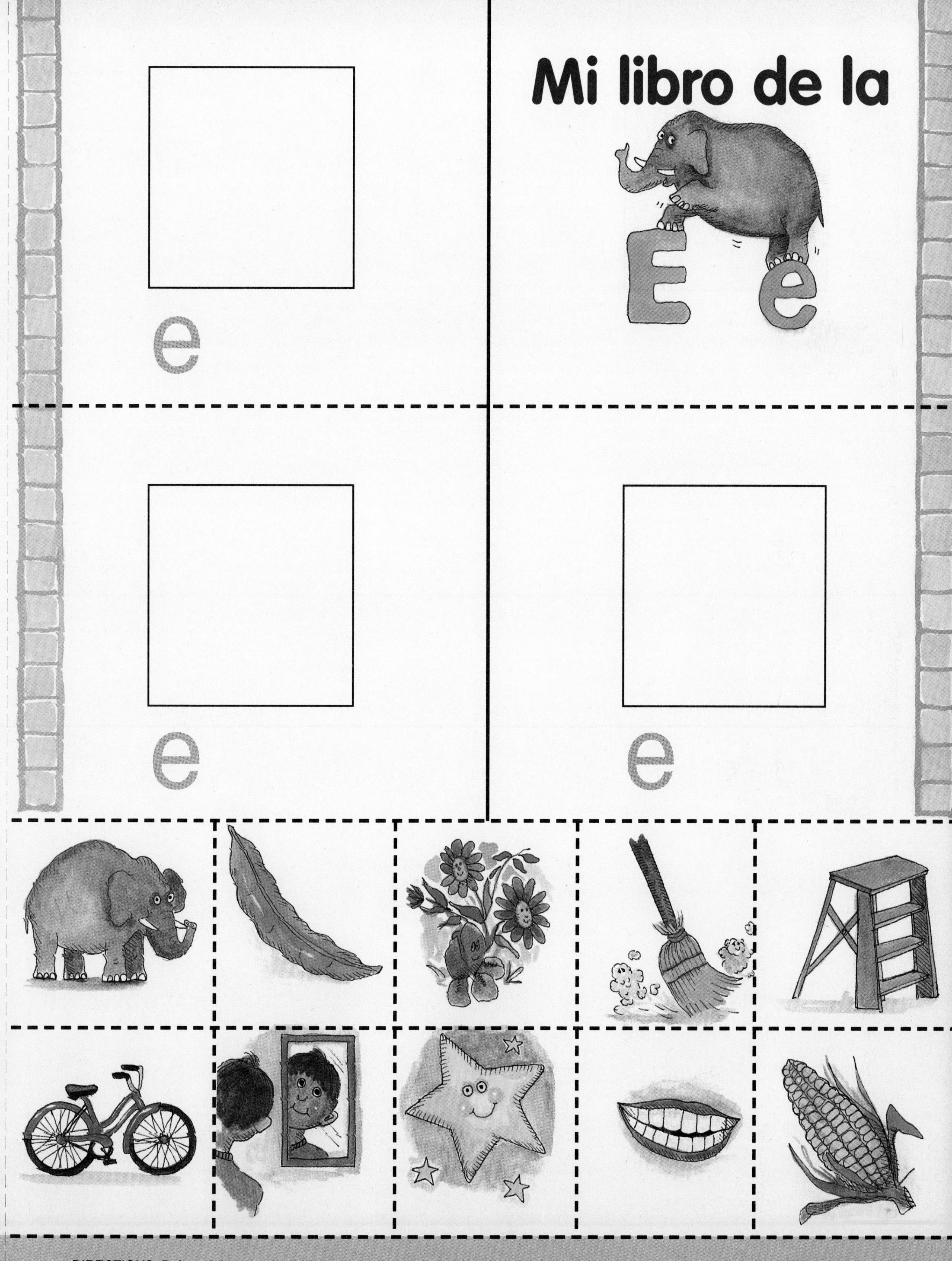

DIRECTIONS: Before children make this picture book, name the pictures: *elefante, ejote, flores, escoba, escalera, bicicleta, espejo, estrella, dientes, elote*. Ask children to paste a picture whose name begins with *e* on each page and to trace the *e* as they say the name of the picture.

e
e
e
e

¡Qué elegantes!

8

Elefantes

por ______________

_____ una fiesta

6

_____ delgado.

3

DIRECTIONS: Children make an eight-page picture book. Have them trace the word *Es* on page 2, and write it on the line on pages 3-6 to complete the sentence. Then read the book with children as they track the print.

Es gordo.

2

de elefantes.

7

_____ verde.

4

_____ morado.

5

U u urraca

Come espinacas.

Escribe U u.

DIRECTIONS: Have children trace the *U-u*, identify the word that begins with *u* and circle the *u*. Then have them practice writing *u* in the box.

Querida familia:

Estamos estudiando la *u*. En el otro lado de esta hoja hay una rima sobre la *u*. Su hijo/a se la puede enseñar y pueden recitarla juntos.

En el siguiente cuadro, dibujen algunas cosas que empiecen con *u*, o peguen fotografías de esos objetos. Luego, completen la oración con el nombre de uno de ellos.

____________ empieza con u.

DIRECTIONS: Have children take this page home and work with their families to draw one or more objects whose names begin with *u*. Then, they complete the sentence with the name of one of them.

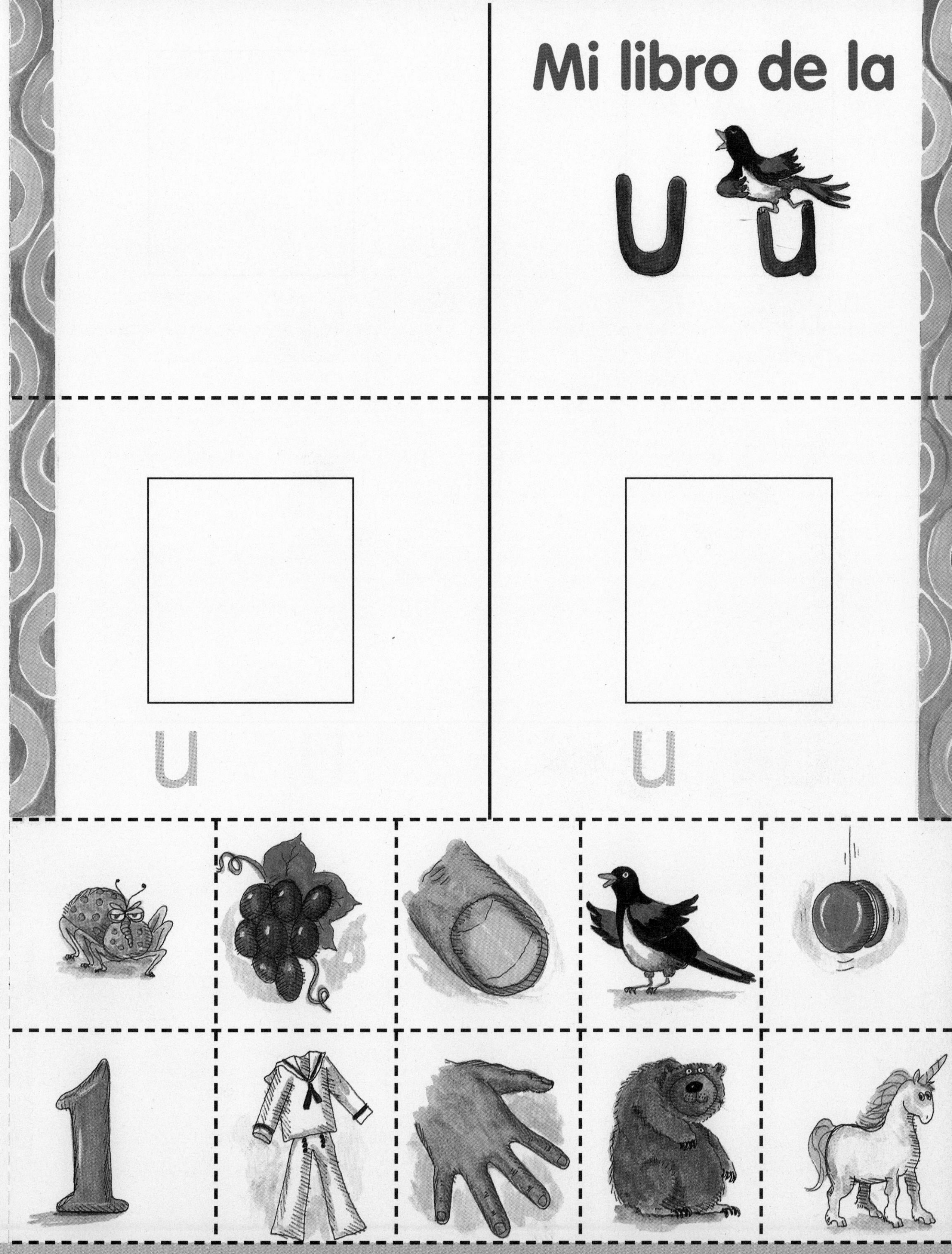

DIRECTIONS: Before children make this picture book, name the pictures: *insecto, uvas, uña, urraca, yoyo, uno, uniforme, mano, oso, unicornio.* Ask children to paste a picture whose name begins with *u* on each page and to trace the *u* as they say the name of the picture.

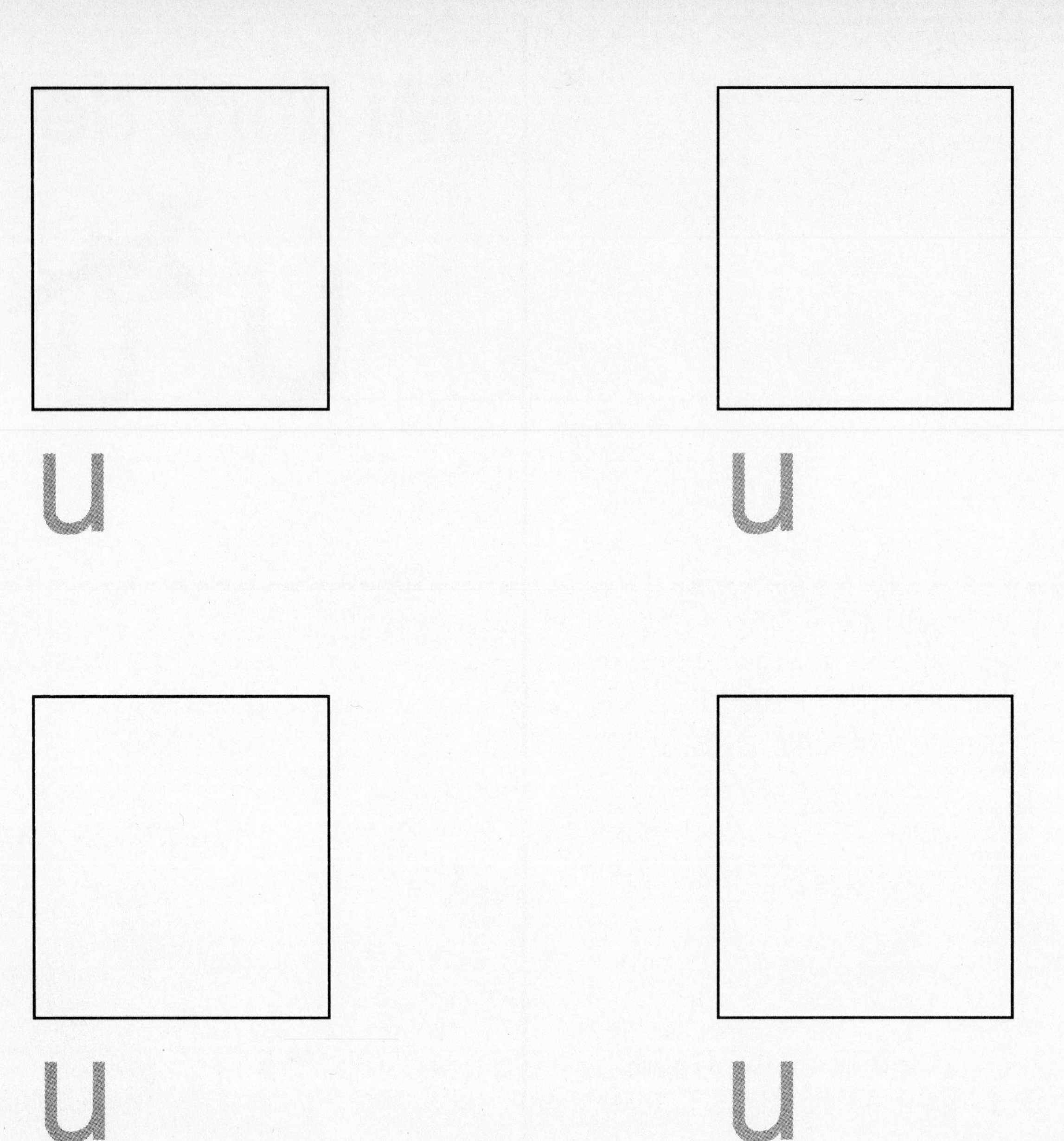
u
u
u
u

¡____ oso!

8

por ____________

____ conejo

6

____ pato

3

DIRECTIONS: Children make an eight-page picture book. Have them trace *un* on page 2 and write *un* on the line on the other pages. Then read the book with children as they track the print.

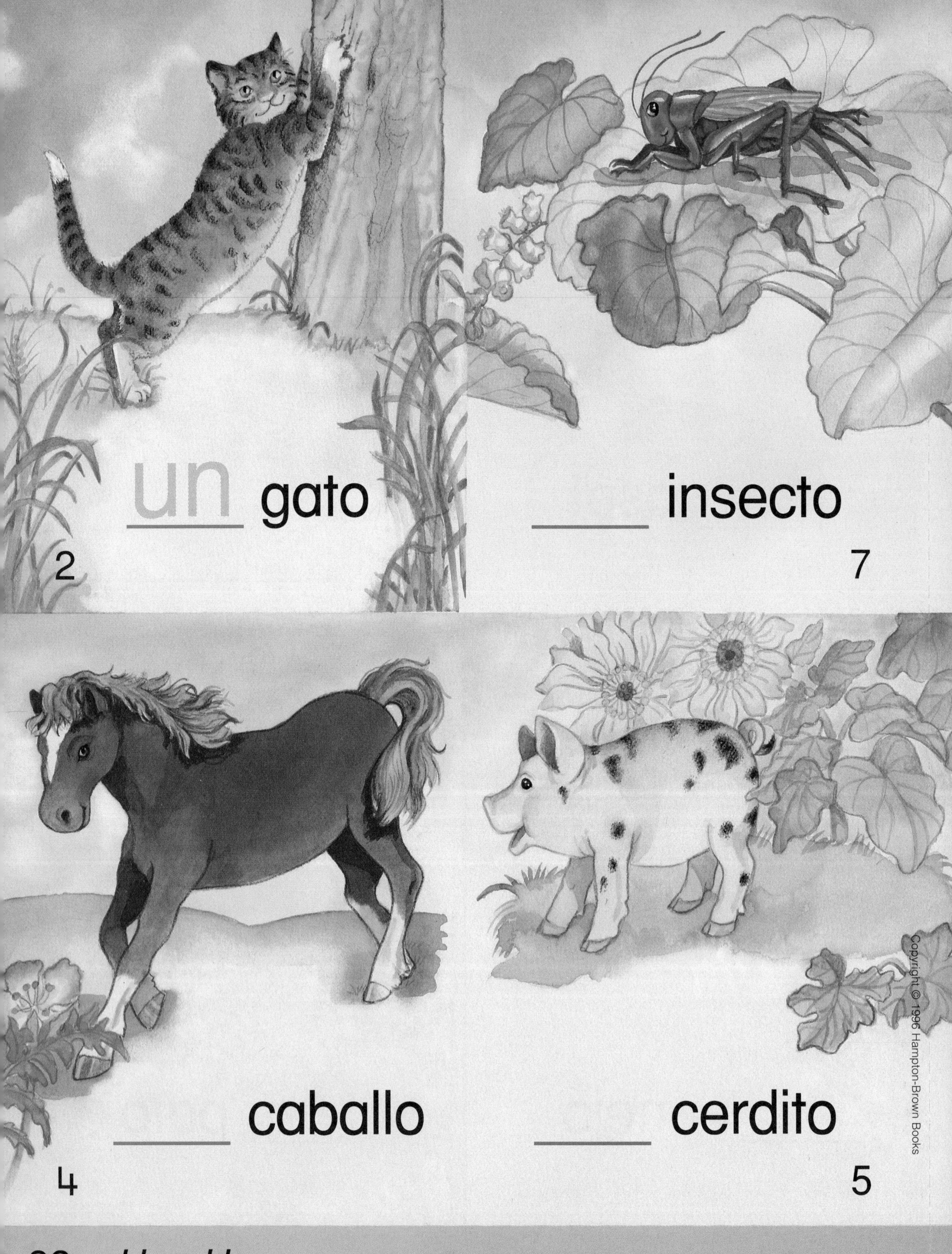
un gato
2
insecto
7
caballo
4
cerdito
5

La marcha de las letras

DIRECTIONS: Have children add more vowels to the parade.

Querida familia:

Estamos repasando las vocales: *a, e, i, o, u.* En el otro lado de esta hoja pueden ver las letras marchando. Pídanle a su hijo/a que les cante la canción *La marcha de las letras.*

En el siguiente cuadro, dibujen una cosa que empiece con cada letra, o peguen un dibujo de ese objeto.

a	e	i	o	u

DIRECTIONS: Have children take this page home and work with their families to draw objects whose names begin with each vowel.

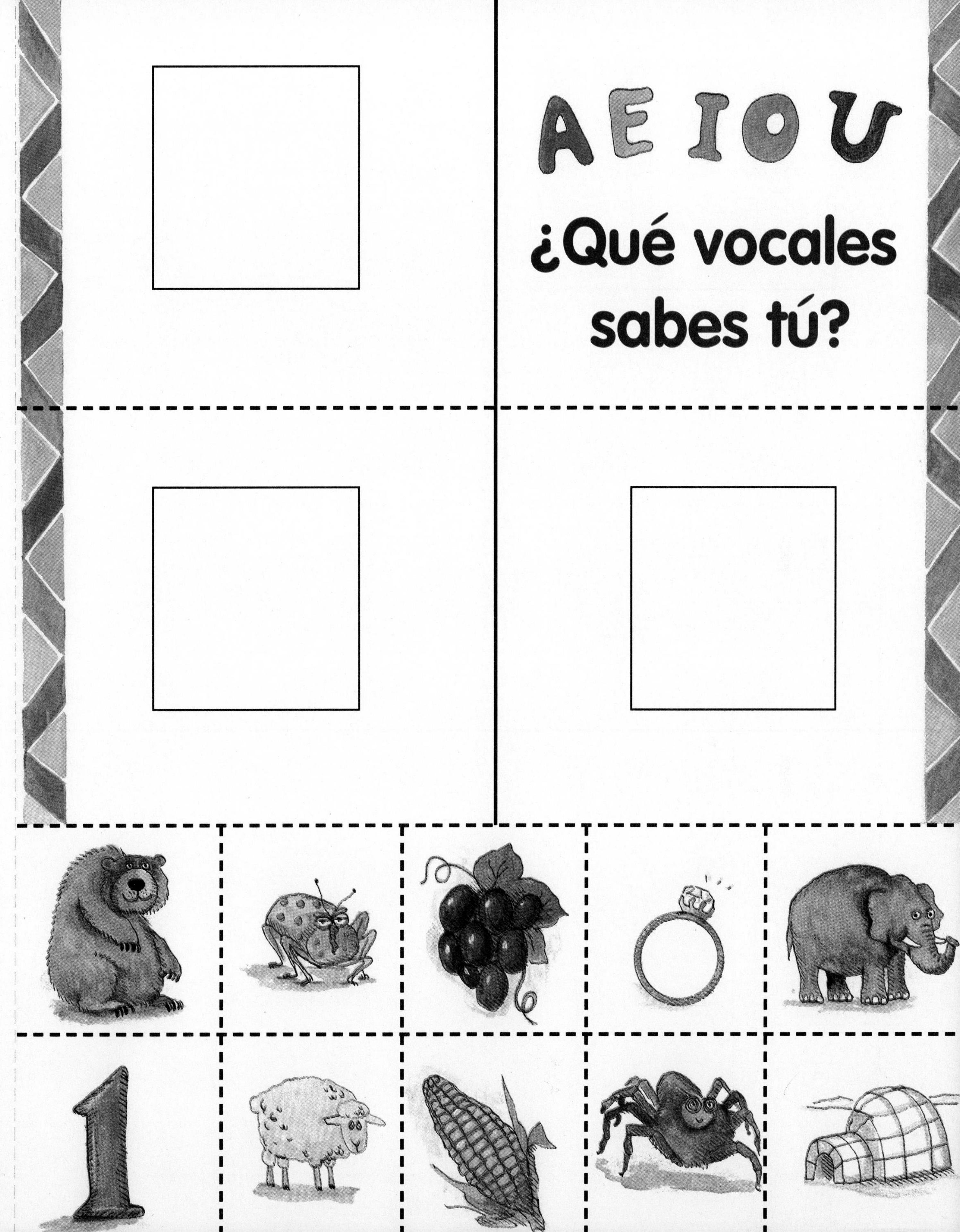

DIRECTIONS: Have children make an eight-page picture book. In each box, ask them to paste or draw pictures whose names begin with a vowel. They can then write the vowel that goes with each picture and take their books home to share with their family.

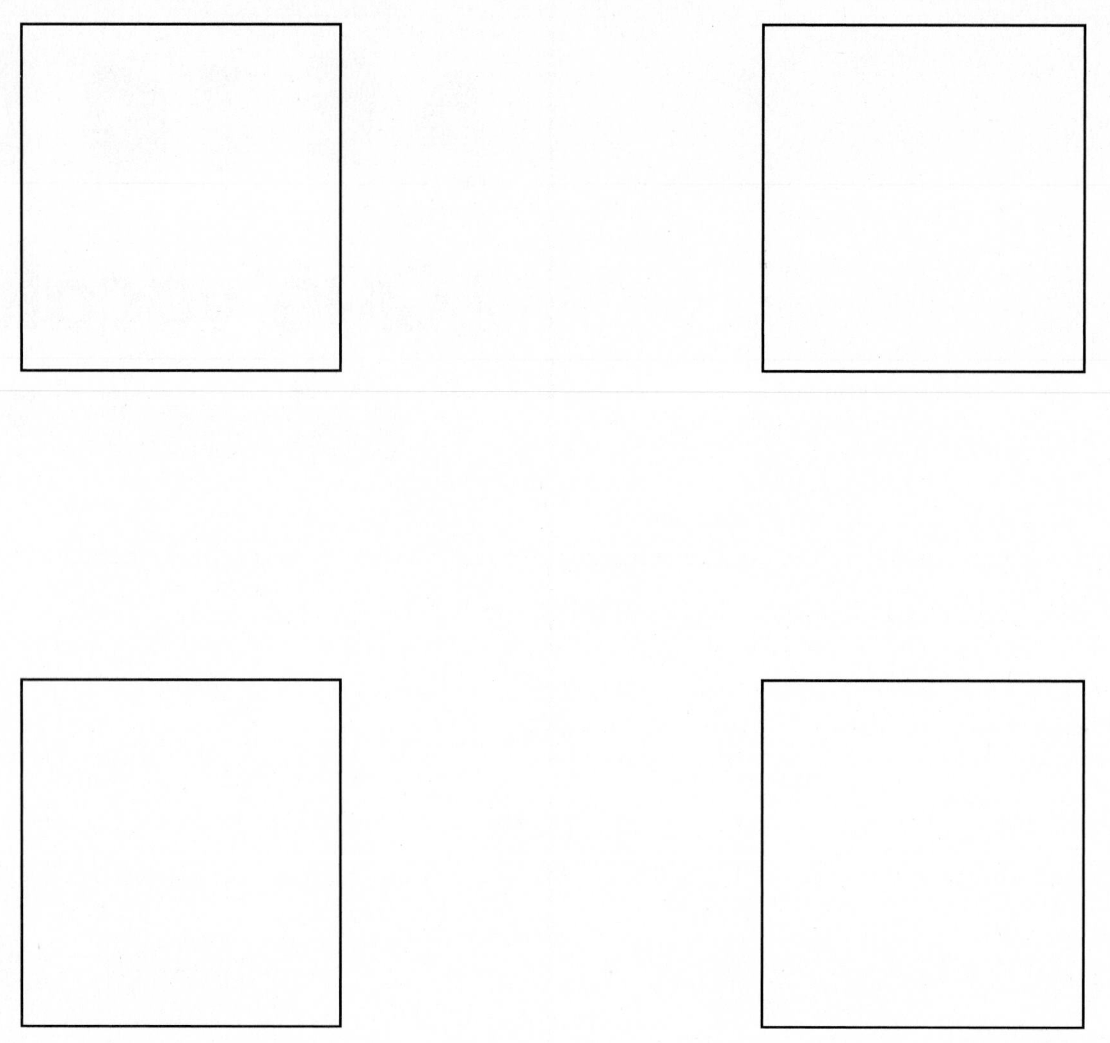

Es la ____
de elefante.

8

Es la ____
de insecto.

6

Es la ____
de ocho.

3

DIRECTIONS: Children make an eight-page picture book, identify the hidden vowel and write it on the line.

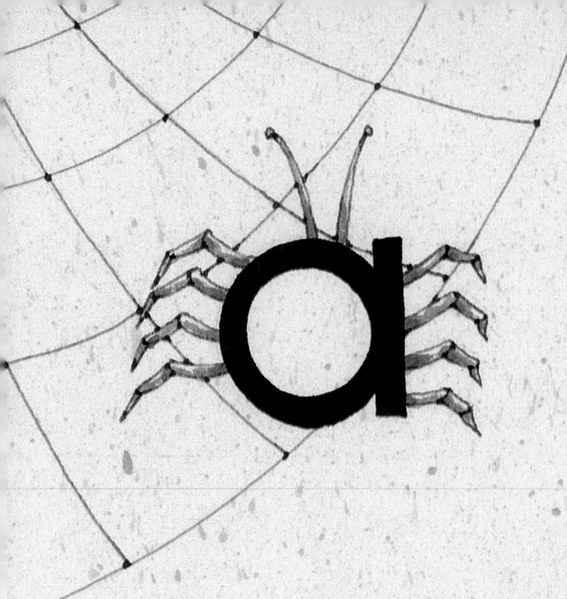

Es la ____
de araña.

2

u

Es la ____
de uña.

7

Es la ____
de oso.

4

Es la ____
de abeja.

5

M m mosquito

Es muy chiquito.

Escribe M m.

DIRECTIONS: Have children trace the *M-m*, identify the words that begin with *m* and circle each *m*. Then have them practice writing *m* in the box.

Querida familia:

Estamos estudiando la *m*. En el otro lado de esta hoja hay una rima sobre la *m*. Su hijo/a se la puede enseñar y pueden recitarla juntos.

En el siguiente cuadro, dibujen algunas cosas que empiecen con *m*, o peguen fotografías de esos objetos. Luego, completen la oración con el nombre de uno de ellos.

____________ empieza con m.

DIRECTIONS: Have children take this page home and work with their families to draw one or more objects whose names begin with *m*. Then, they complete the sentence with the name of one of them.

DIRECTIONS: Before children make this picture book, name the pictures: *muñeca, unicornio, mano, mariposa, mesa, manzana, martillo, molino, impermeable, uña.* Ask children to paste a picture whose name begins with *m* on each page. They can then trace the *m* as they say the name of the object. Some children may also want to write the rest of the word.

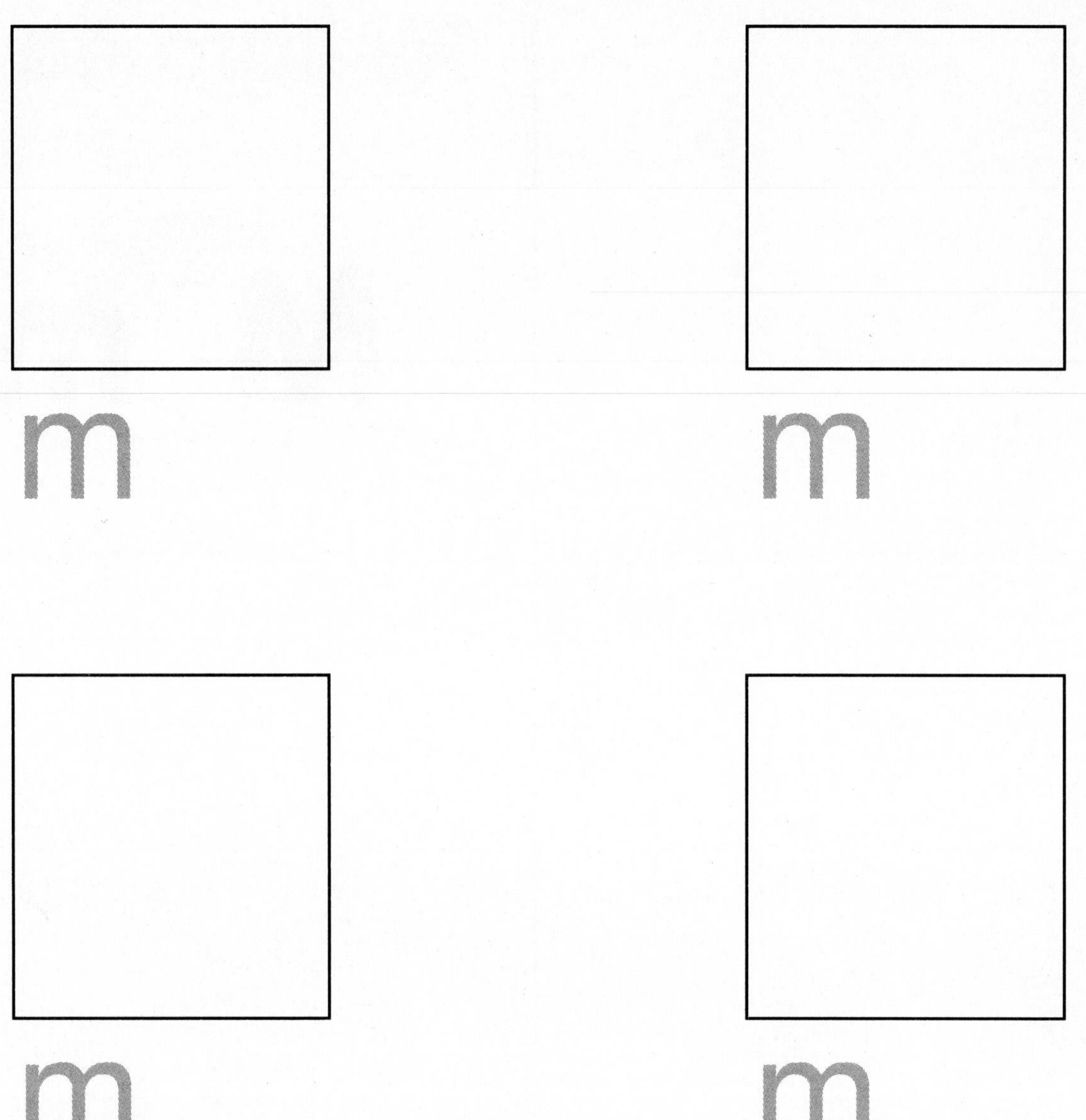
m
m
m
m

8

Mi mamá

por ___________

6

3

DIRECTIONS: Children make an eight-page picture book. Ask them to trace *mi mamá* in the speech balloon on page 2, and to write *mi mamá* in the speech balloons on the other pages to show what each baby is saying to its mother. Then read the book as children track the print. Ask them to speculate on who is the mother of the new baby on page 8.

mi
mamá
2
7
4
5

P p pato

Se pone un zapato.

Escribe P p.

DIRECTIONS: Have children trace the *P-p*, identify the words that begin with *p* and circle each *p*. Then have them practice writing *p* in the box.

Querida familia:

Estamos estudiando la *p*. En el otro lado de esta hoja hay una rima sobre la *p*. Su hijo/a se la puede enseñar y pueden recitarla juntos.

En el siguiente cuadro, dibujen algunas cosas que empiecen con *p*, o peguen fotografías de esos objetos. Luego, completen la oración con el nombre de uno de ellos.

_____________ empieza con p.

DIRECTIONS: Have children take this page home and work with their families to draw one or more objects whose names begin with *p*. Then, they complete the sentence with the name of one of them.

DIRECTIONS: Before children make this picture book, name the pictures: *león, pájaro, pelota, pato, dos, patines, pingüino, perro, piñata, luna*. Ask children to make an eight-page picture book. Ask them to paste a picture whose name begins with *p* on each page. They can then trace the *p* as they say the name of the object. Some children may also want to write the rest of the word.

p

p

p

p

DIRECTIONS: Children make an eight-page picture book. Have them trace *papá* in the speech balloon on page 2, and write *papá* in the speech balloons on the other pages. Then read the book as children track the print.

papá
2
7
4
5

T t toro

Habla como un loro.

Escribe T t.

DIRECTIONS: Have children trace the *T-t*, identify the word that begins with *t* and circle the *t*. Then have them practice writing *t* in the box.

Querida familia:

Estamos estudiando la *t*. En el otro lado de esta hoja hay una rima sobre la *t*. Su hijo/a se la puede enseñar y pueden recitarla juntos.

En el siguiente cuadro, dibujen algunas cosas que empiecen con *t*, o peguen fotografías de esos objetos. Luego, completen la oración con el nombre de uno de ellos.

_______________ empieza con t.

DIRECTIONS: Have children take this page home and work with their families to draw one or more objects whose names begin with *t*. Then, they complete the sentence with the name of one of them.

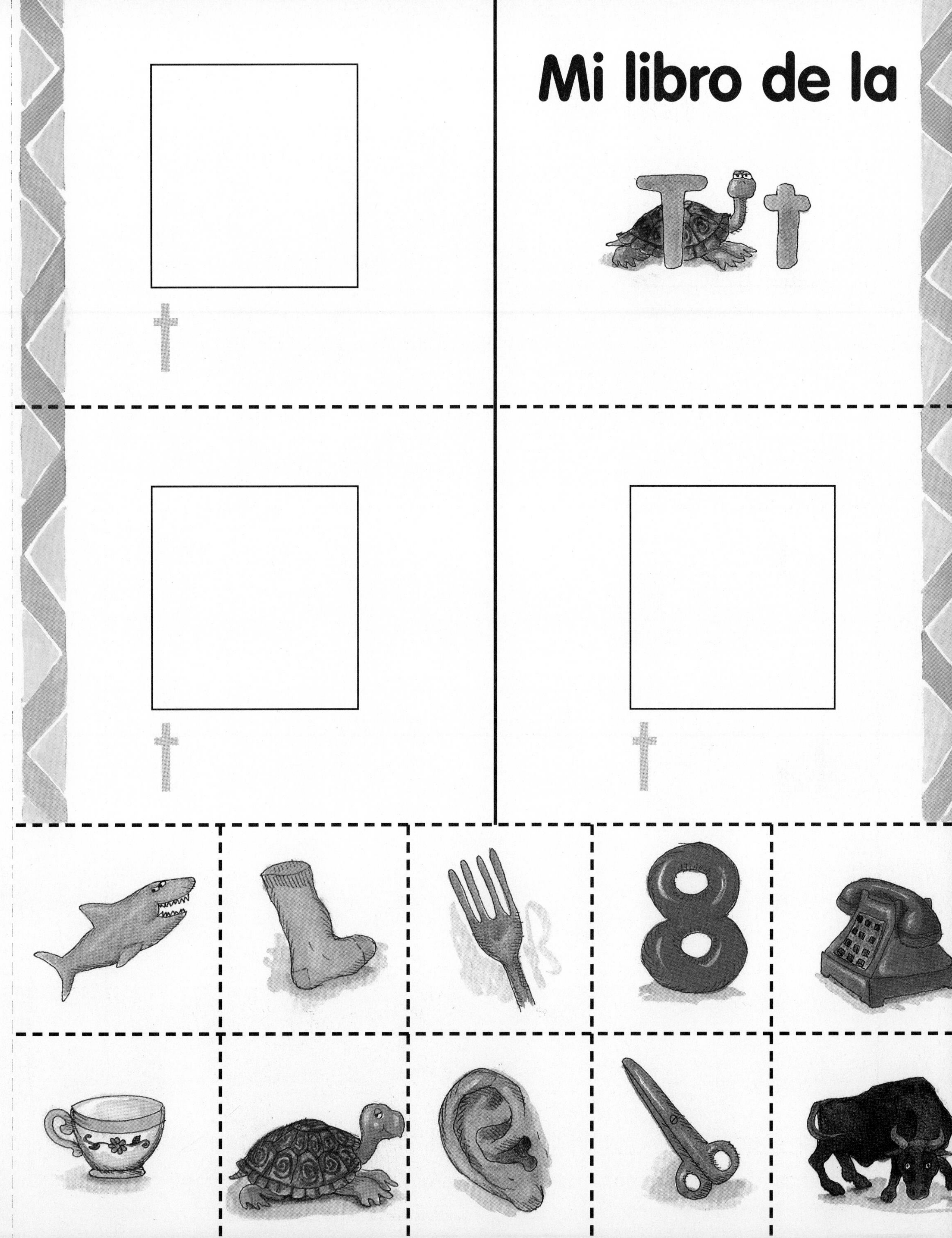

DIRECTIONS: Before children make this picture book, name the pictures: *tiburón, calcetín, tenedor, ocho, teléfono, taza, tortuga, oreja, tijeras, toro.* Ask children to paste a picture whose name begins with *t* on each page. They can then trace the *t* as they say the name of the object. Some children may also want to write the rest of the word.

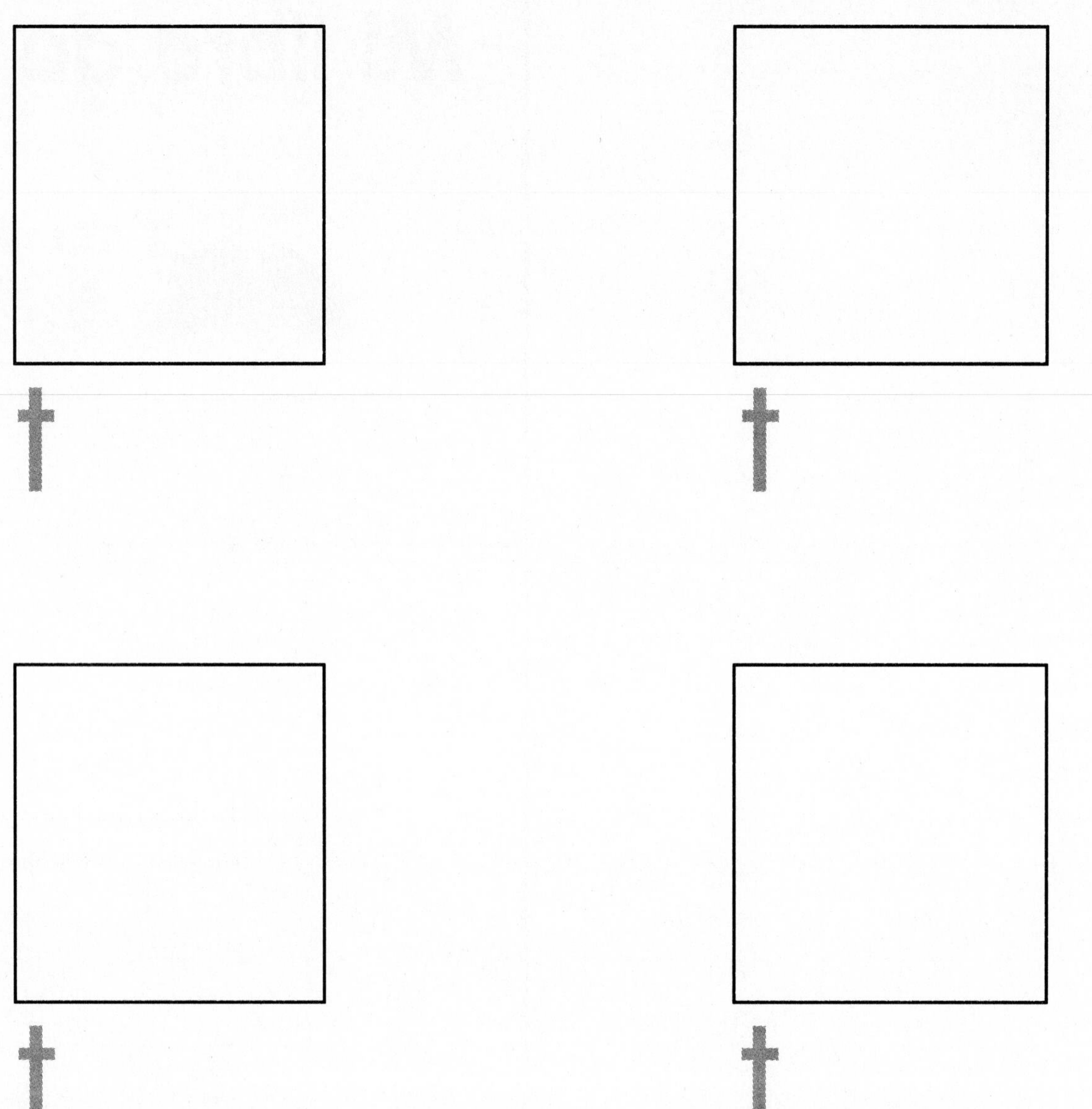

8

¡A nadar!

por ____________

6

3

DIRECTIONS: Have children make an eight-page picture book. Ask them to trace *tú* in the speech balloon on page 2, and write *tú* in the speech balloons on the other pages.

tú
2
7
4
5

S s sapo

Eres muy guapo.

Escribe S s.

DIRECTIONS: Have children trace the *S-s*, identify the word that begins with *s* and circle the *s*. Then have them practice writing *s* in the box.

Querida familia:

Estamos estudiando la *s*. En el otro lado de esta hoja hay una rima sobre la *s*. Su hijo/a se la puede enseñar y pueden recitarla juntos.

En el siguiente cuadro, dibujen algunas cosas que empiecen con *s*, o peguen fotografías de esos objetos. Luego, completen la oración con el nombre de uno de ellos.

__________ empieza con s.

DIRECTIONS: Have children take this page home and work with their families to draw one or more objects whose names begin with *s*. Then, they complete the sentence with the name of one of them.

DIRECTIONS: Before children make this picture book, name the pictures: *sapo, silla, fresa, sofá, seis, sombrero, sol, sandía, rosa, arco iris.* Ask children to paste a picture whose name begins with *s* on each page. They can then trace the *s* as they say the name of the object. Some children may also want to write the rest of the word.

s

s

s

s

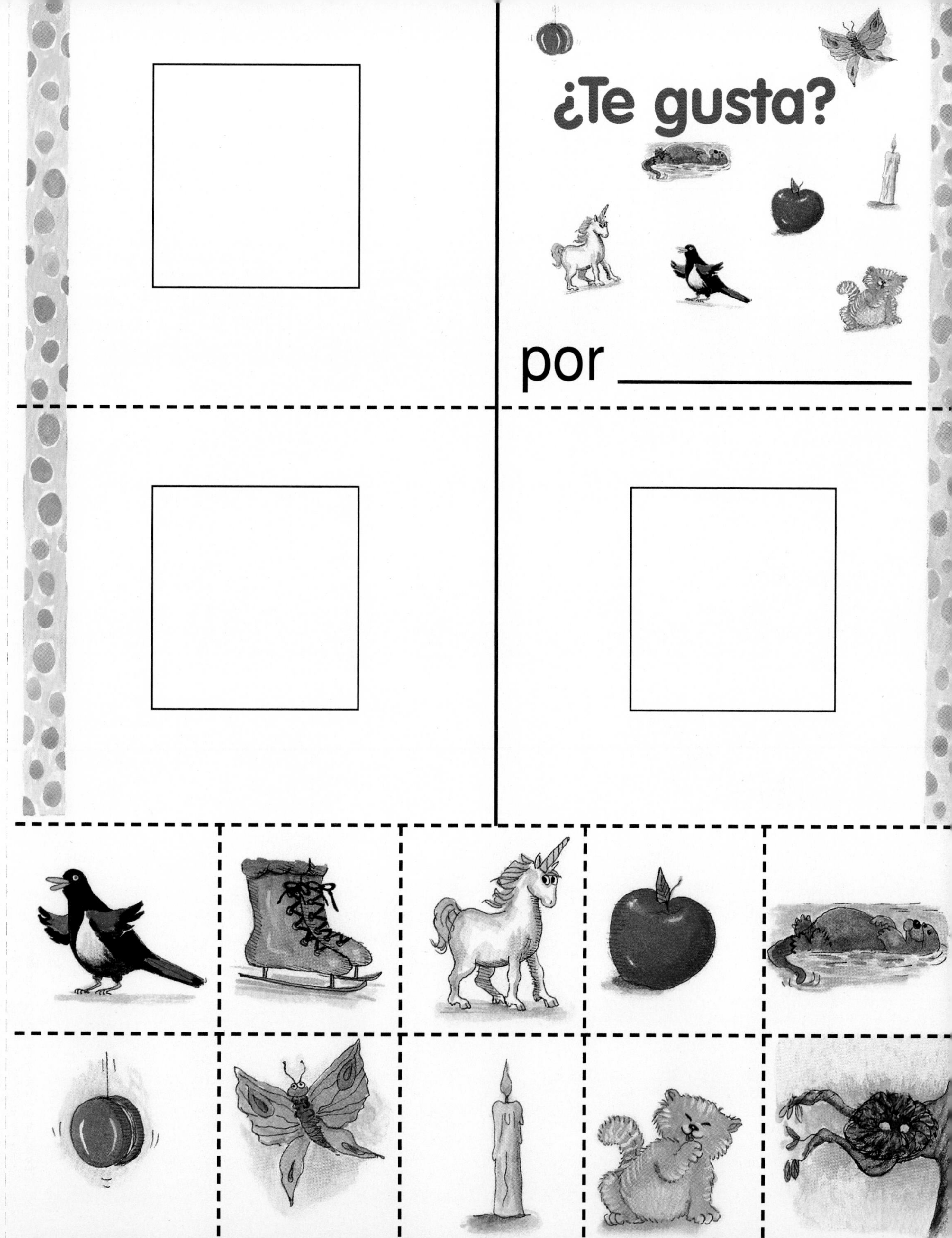

DIRECTIONS: Before children make this picture book, name the pictures: *urraca, patines, unicornio, manzana, nutria, yoyo, mariposa, vela, gato, nido.* Ask children to paste in pictures of things they like, trace *sí*, and write *sí* under the other pictures. Partners can then share their books and discuss their choices.

sí

L l lombriz

No tienes nariz.

Escribe L l.

DIRECTIONS: Have children trace the *L-l*, identify the word that begins with *l* and circle the *l*. Then have them practice writing *l* in the box.

Querida familia:

Estamos estudiando la *l*. En el otro lado de esta hoja hay una rima sobre la *l*. Su hijo/a se la puede enseñar y pueden recitarla juntos.

En el siguiente cuadro, dibujen algunas cosas que empiecen con *l*, o peguen fotografías de esos objetos. Luego, completen la oración con el nombre de uno de ellos.

____________ empieza con l.

DIRECTIONS: Have children take this page home and work with their families to draw one or more objects whose names begin with *l*. Then, they complete the sentence with the name of one of them.

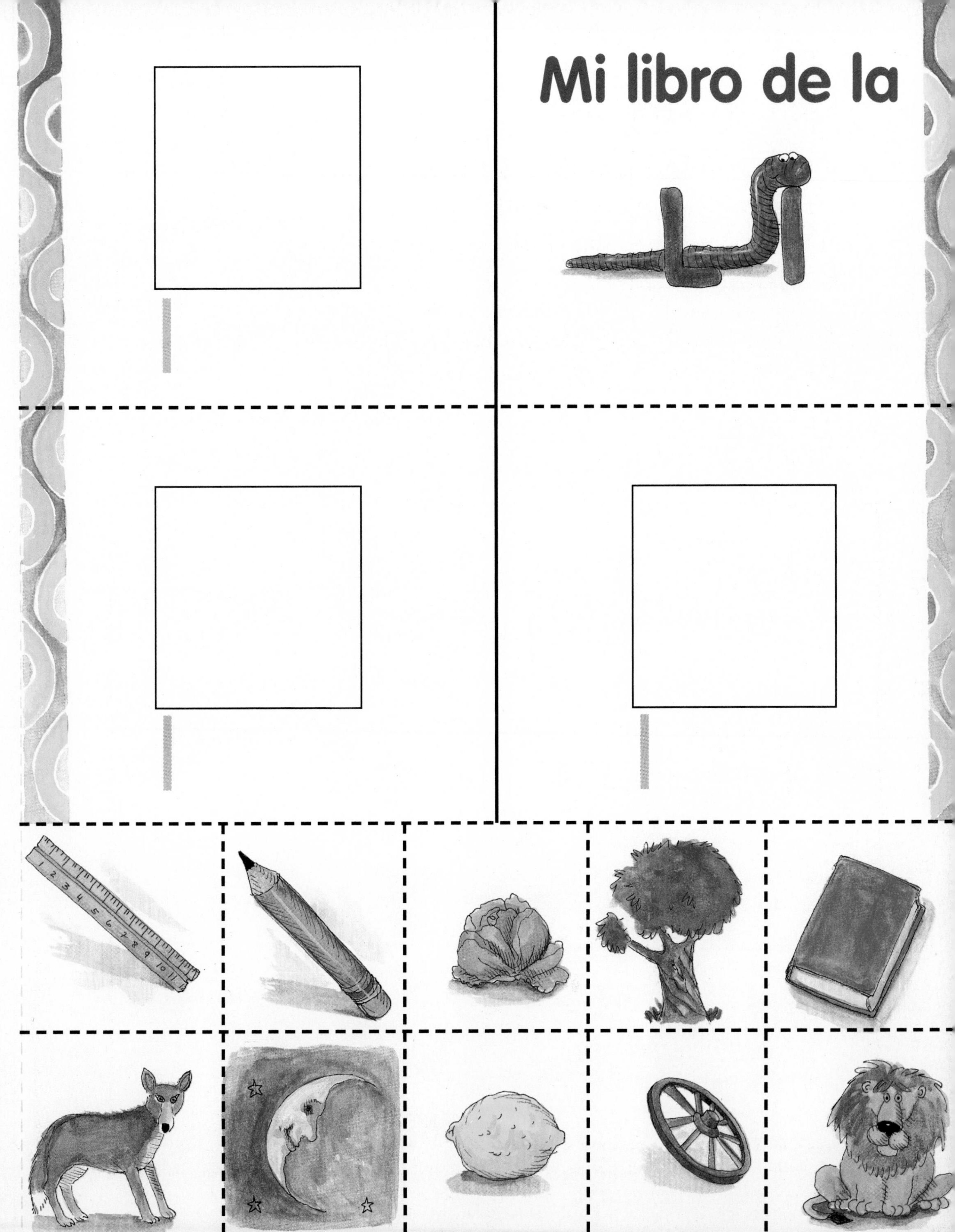

DIRECTIONS: Before children make this picture book, name the pictures: *regla, lápiz, lechuga, árbol, libro, lobo, luna, limón, rueda, león.* Ask children to paste a picture whose name begins with *l* on each page. They can then trace the *l* as they say the name of the object. Some children may also want to write the rest of the word.

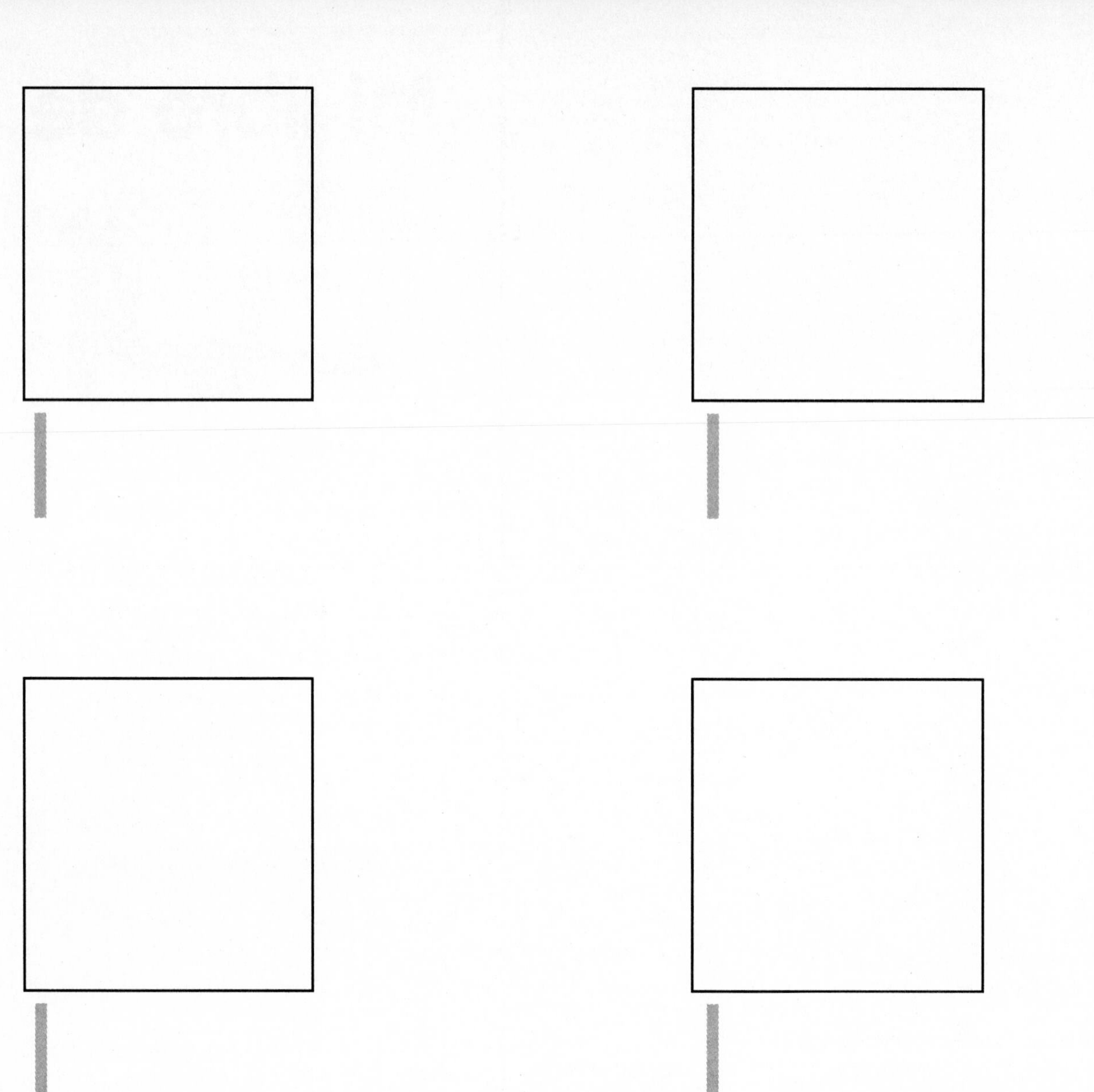

____ granja

8

La granja

por ____________

____ tortuga

6

____ gallina

3

DIRECTIONS: Children make an eight-page picture book. Have them trace *la* on page 2 and write *la* on the line on the other pages. Read the book with children as they track the print.

la lombriz

2

___ pata

7

___ abeja

4

___ araña

5

V v vaca

No es muy flaca.

Escribe V v.

DIRECTIONS: Have children trace the *V-v*, identify the word that begins with *v* and circle the *v*. Then have them practice writing *v* in the box.

Querida familia:

Estamos estudiando la *v*. En el otro lado de esta hoja hay una rima sobre la *v*. Su hijo/a se la puede enseñar y pueden recitarla juntos.

En el siguiente cuadro, dibujen algunas cosas que empiecen con *v*, o peguen fotografías de esos objetos. Luego, completen la oración con el nombre de uno de ellos.

__________ empieza con v.

DIRECTIONS: Have children take this page home and work with their families to draw one or more objects whose names begin with *v*. Then, they complete the sentence with the name of one of them.

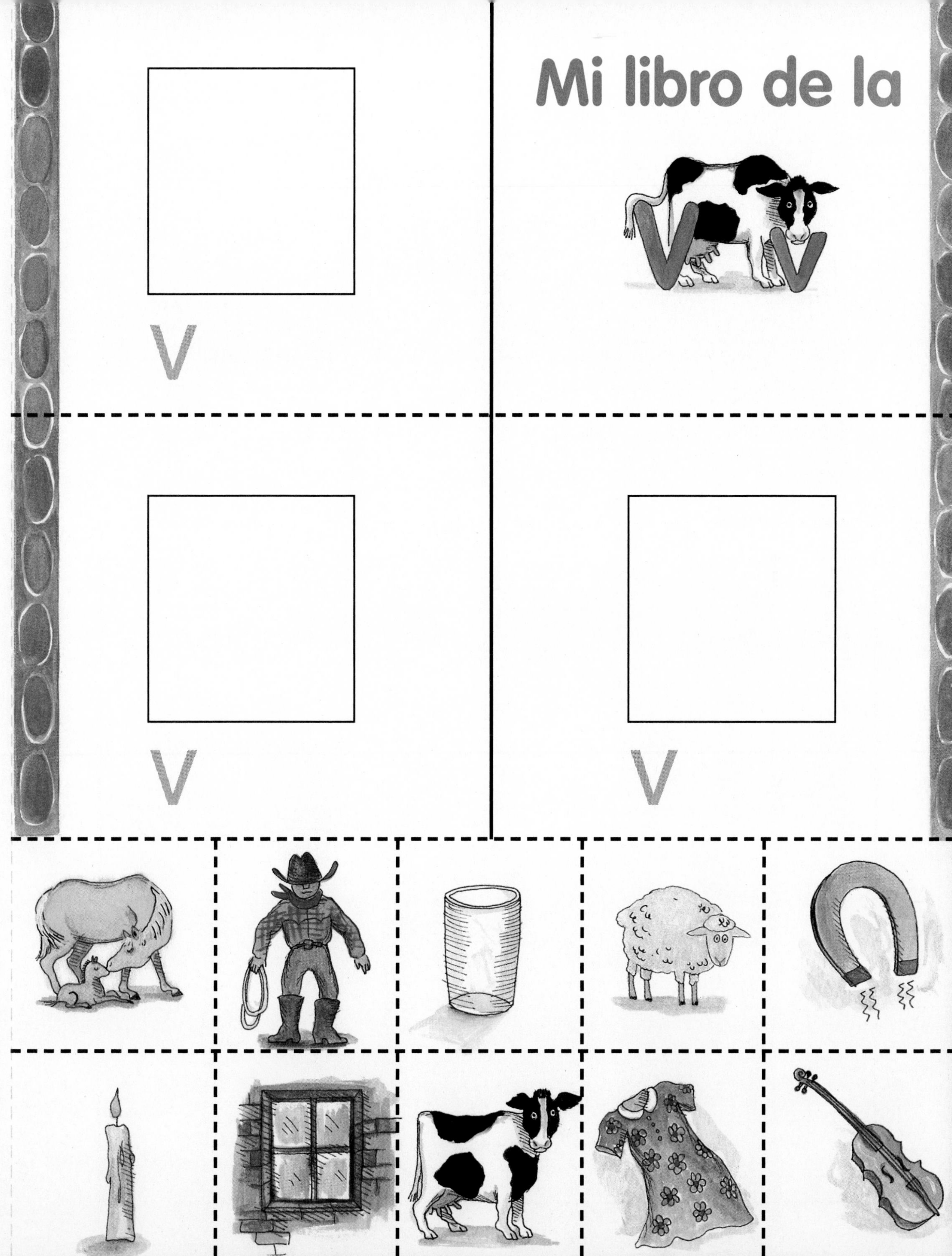

DIRECTIONS: Before children make this picture book, name the pictures: *yegua, vaquero, vaso, oveja, imán, vela, ventana, vaca, vestido, violín.* Ask children to paste a picture whose name begins with *v* on each page. They can then trace the *v* as they say the name of the object. Some children may also want to write the rest of the word.

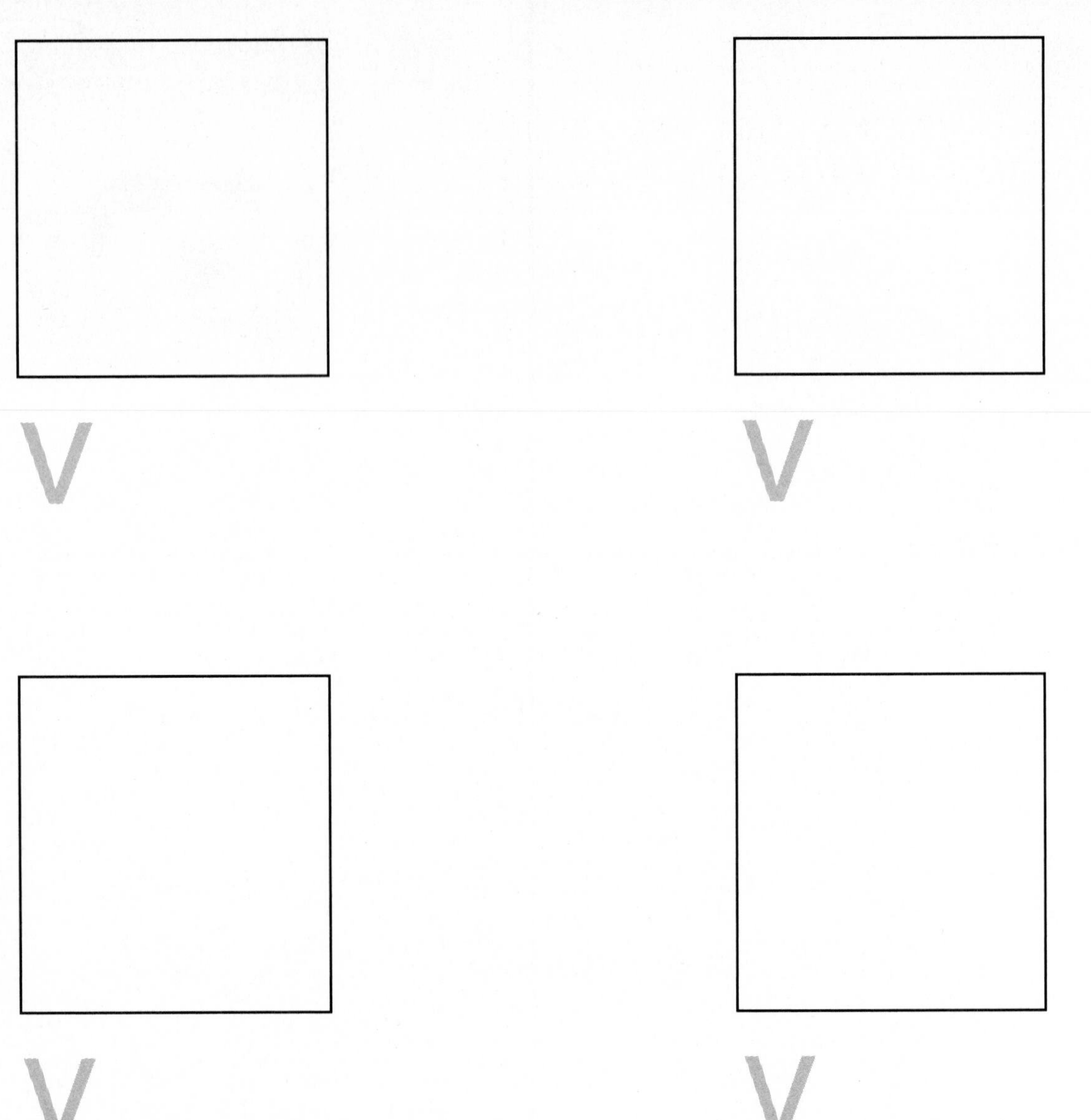

Veo, veo

por ______________

______ un pato.

3

______ un loro.

5

DIRECTIONS: Children make a six-page picture book. Have them trace *Veo* on page 2 and write *Veo* on the line on the other pages to complete the sentence. Read the book with children as they track the print.

Veo un sapo.

2

_______ un toro.

4

_______ una vaca con maracas.

6

F f foca

Se sienta en la roca.

Escribe F f.

DIRECTIONS: Have children trace the *F-f*, identify the word that begins with *f* and circle the *f*. Then have them practice writing *f* in the box.

Querida familia:

Estamos estudiando la *f*. En el otro lado de esta hoja hay una rima sobre la *f*. Su hijo/a se la puede enseñar y pueden recitarla juntos.

En el siguiente cuadro, dibujen algunas cosas que empiecen con *f*, o peguen fotografías de esos objetos. Luego, completen la oración con el nombre de uno de ellos.

____________ empieza con f.

DIRECTIONS: Have children take this page home and work with their families to draw one or more objects whose names begin with *f*. Then, they complete the sentence with the name of one of them.

DIRECTIONS: Before children make this picture book, name the pictures: *delfín, faro, foca, flores, abeja, foto, fresa, silla, fruta, falda.* Ask children to paste a picture whose name begins with *f* on each page. They can then trace the *f* as they say the name of the object. Some children may also want to write the rest of the word.

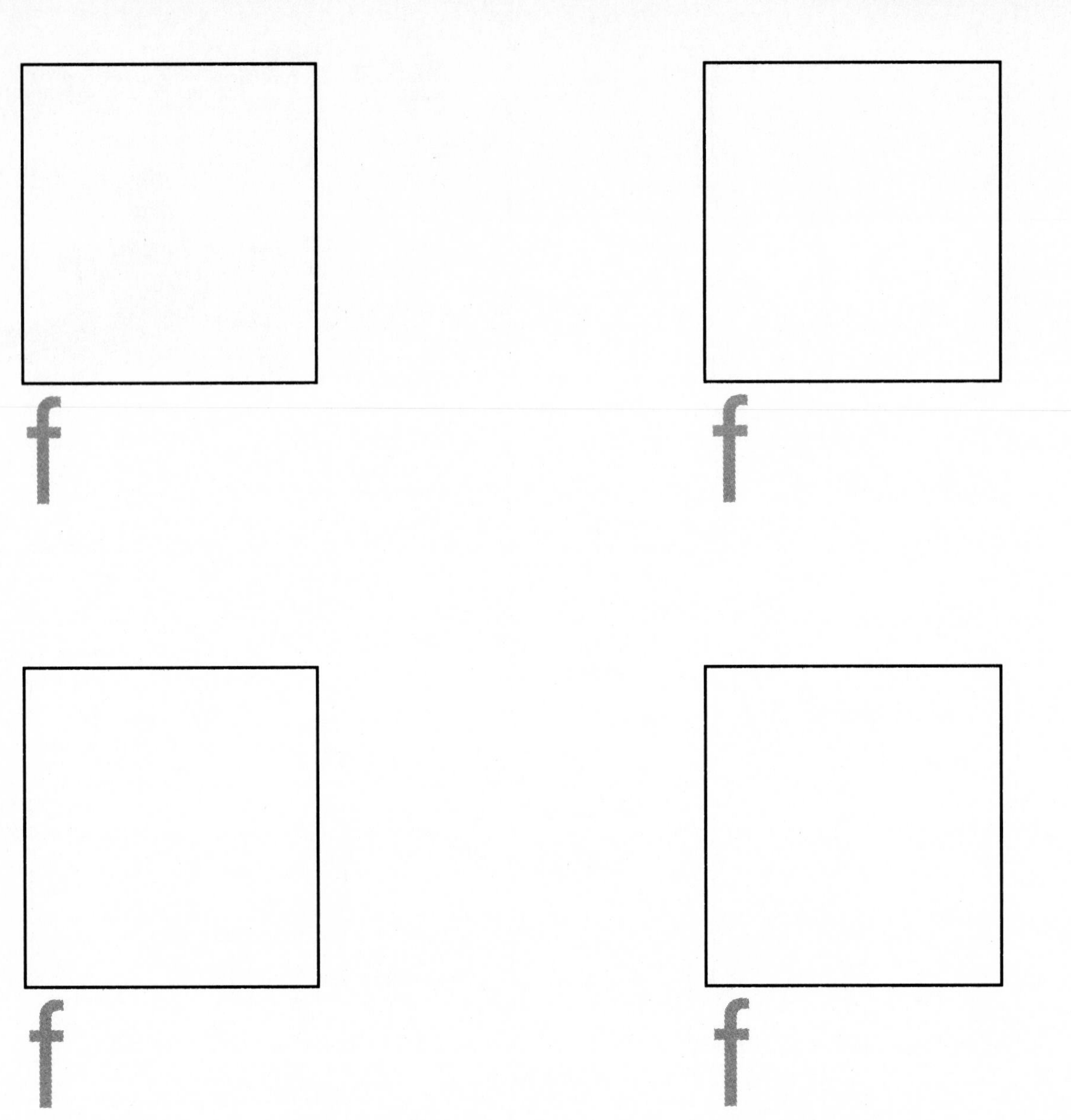
f
f
f
f

¿Adónde fue?

por ___________

______ a la tina.

3

______ a la playa.

5

DIRECTIONS: Children make a six-page picture book. Have them trace *Fue* on page 2 and write *Fue* on the line on the other pages to complete the sentence. Read the book with children as they track the print.

Fue a la escuela.

2

_______ al cine.

4

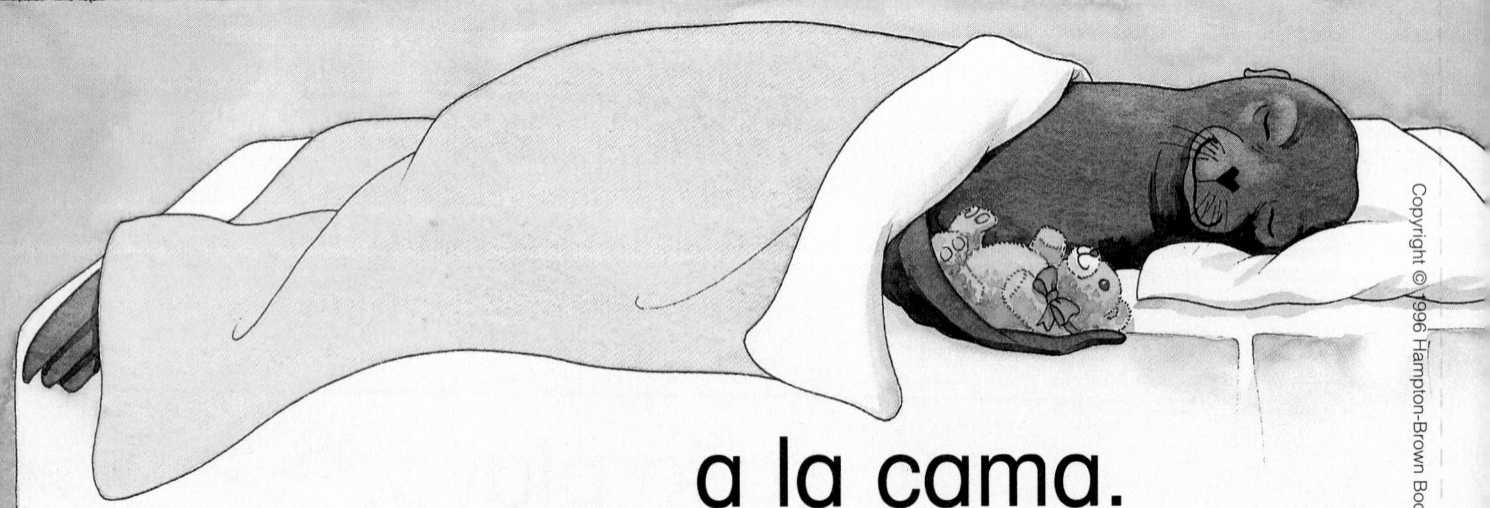

_______ a la cama.

6

Y y yegua

¿A qué hora llega?

Escribe Y y.

DIRECTIONS: Have children trace the *Y-y*, identify the word that begins with *y* and circle the *y*. Then have them practice writing *y* in the box.

Querida familia:

Estamos estudiando la y. En el otro lado de esta hoja hay una rima sobre la y. Su hijo/a se la puede enseñar y pueden recitarla juntos.

En el siguiente cuadro, dibujen algunas cosas que empiecen con y, o peguen fotografías de esos objetos. Luego, completen la oración con el nombre de uno de ellos.

_____________ empieza con y.

DIRECTIONS: Have children take this page home and work with their families to draw one or more objects whose names begin with *y*. Then, they complete the sentence with the name of one of them.

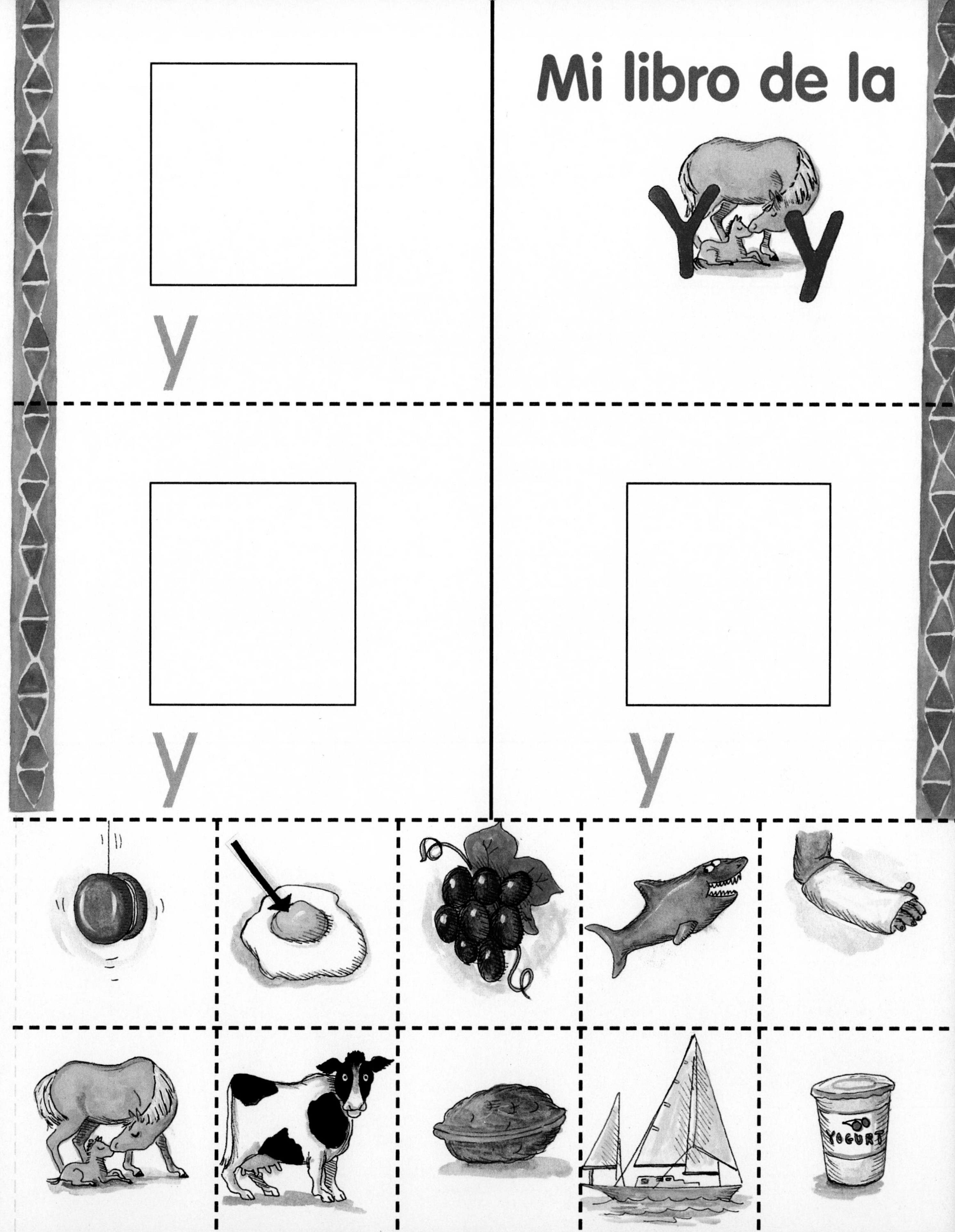

DIRECTIONS: Before children make this picture book, name the pictures: *yoyo, yema, uvas, tiburón, yeso, yegua, vaca, nuez, yate, yogur.* Ask children to paste a picture whose name begins with *y* on each page. They can then trace the *y* as they say the name of the object. Some children may also want to write the rest of the word.

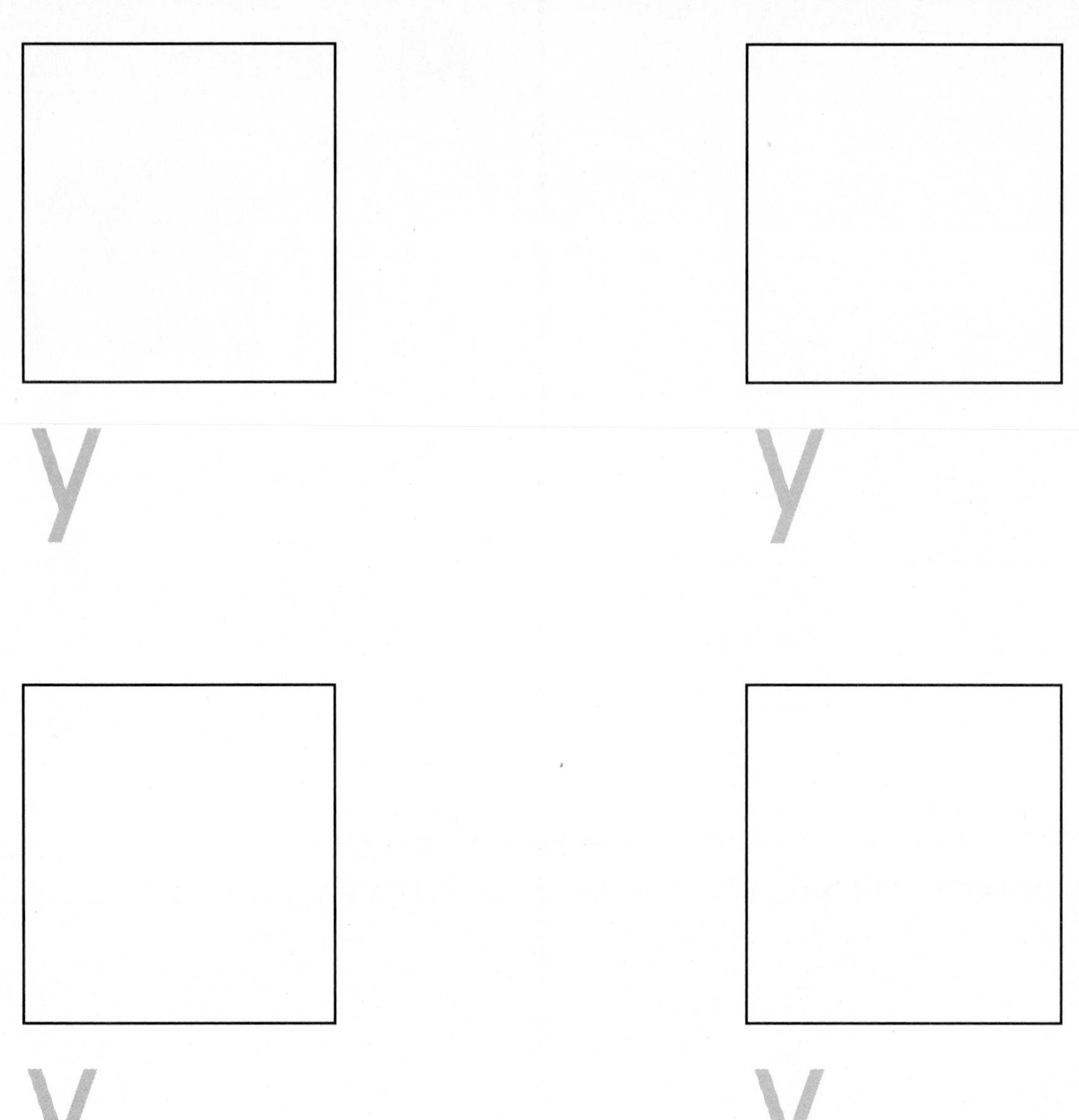
y
y
y
y

8

¿Quién quiere un paraguas?

por ____________

6

3

DIRECTIONS: Children make an eight-page picture book. Have them trace *Yo* on page 2 and write *Yo* in the speech balloons on the other pages. Read the book with children as they track the print.

Yo
2
7
4
5

J j jirafa

No es muy baja.

Escribe J j.

DIRECTIONS: Have children trace the *J-j*, identify the word that begins with *j* and circle the *j*. Then have them practice writing *j* in the box.

Querida familia:

Estamos estudiando la *j*. En el otro lado de esta hoja hay una rima sobre la *j*. Su hijo/a se la puede enseñar y pueden recitarla juntos.

En el siguiente cuadro, dibujen algunas cosas que empiecen con *j*, o peguen fotografías de esos objetos. Luego, completen la oración con el nombre de uno de ellos.

______________ empieza con j.

DIRECTIONS: Have children take this page home and work with their families to draw one or more objects whose names begin with *j*. Then, they complete the sentence with the name of one of them.

DIRECTIONS: Before children make this picture book, name the pictures: *juguetes, jirafa, jabón, limón, jugo, jamón, insecto, jarra, jaula, falda.* Ask children to paste a picture whose name begins with *j* on each page. They can then trace the *j* as they say the name of the object. Some children may also want to write the rest of the word.

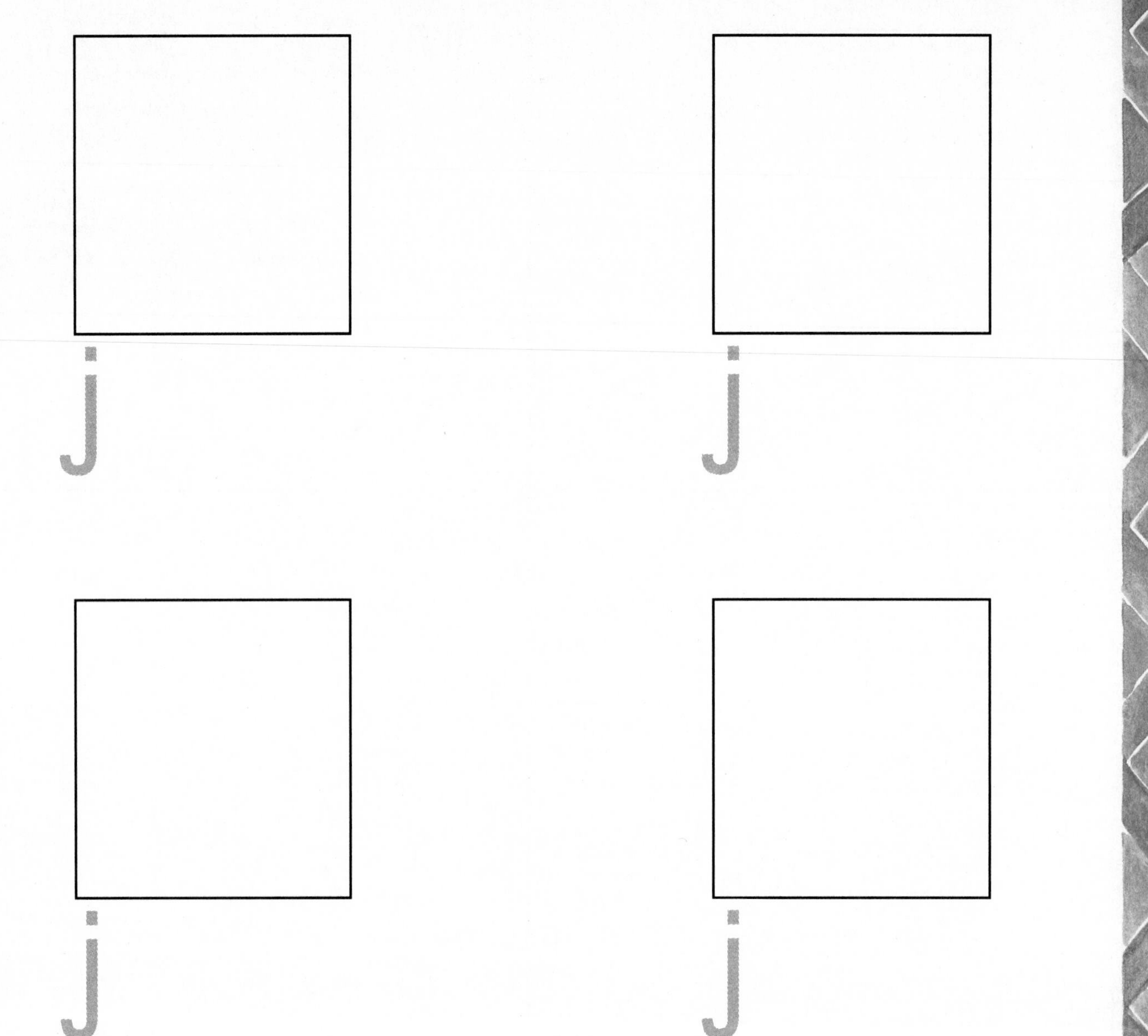
j
j
j
j

por ______________

______________ con canicas.

3

______________ con el perro.

5

DIRECTIONS: Children make a six-page picture book. Have them trace *Juego* on page 2 and write *Juego* on the line on the other pages to complete the sentence. Read the book with children as they track the print.

Juego con la pelota.

2

_______ con mis carritos.

4

_______ con mis amigos.

6

G g gato

Baila todo el rato.

Escribe G g.

DIRECTIONS: Have children trace the *G-g*, identify the word that begins with *g* and circle the *g*. Then have them practice writing *g* in the box.

Querida familia:

Estamos estudiando la *g*. En el otro lado de esta hoja hay una rima sobre la *g*. Su hijo/a se la puede enseñar y pueden recitarla juntos.

En el siguiente cuadro, dibujen algunas cosas que empiecen con *g*, o peguen fotografías de esos objetos. Luego, completen la oración con el nombre de uno de ellos.

____________ empieza con g.

DIRECTIONS: Have children take this page home and work with their families to draw one or more objects whose names begin with *g*. Then, they complete the sentence with the name of one of them.

DIRECTIONS: Before children make this picture book, name the pictures: *oruga, gato, guante, conejo, gallina, guitarra, gusano, gorra, gorila, tenedor.* Ask children to paste a picture whose name begins with *g* on each page. They can then trace the *g* as they say the name of the object. Some children may also want to write the rest of the word.

g

g

g

g

¿Qué te gusta?

por ___________

___________ la sandía.

3

___________ la piña.

5

DIRECTIONS: Children make a six-page picture book. Have them trace *Me gusta* on page 2 and write *Me gusta* on the line on the other pages to complete the sentence. Read the book with children as they track the print.

Me gusta el plátano.

2

_______________ el mango.

4

_______________ compartir.

6

D d delfín

Es muy saltarín.

Escribe D d.

DIRECTIONS: Have children trace the *D-d*, identify the word that begins with *d* and circle the *d*. Then have them practice writing *d* in the box.

Querida familia:

Estamos estudiando la *d*. En el otro lado de esta hoja hay una rima sobre la *d*. Su hijo/a se la puede enseñar y pueden recitarla juntos.

En el siguiente cuadro, dibujen algunas cosas que empiecen con *d*, o peguen fotografías de esos objetos. Luego, completen la oración con el nombre de uno de ellos.

________________ empieza con d.

DIRECTIONS: Have children take this page home and work with their families to draw one or more objects whose names begin with *d*. Then, they complete the sentence with the name of one of them.

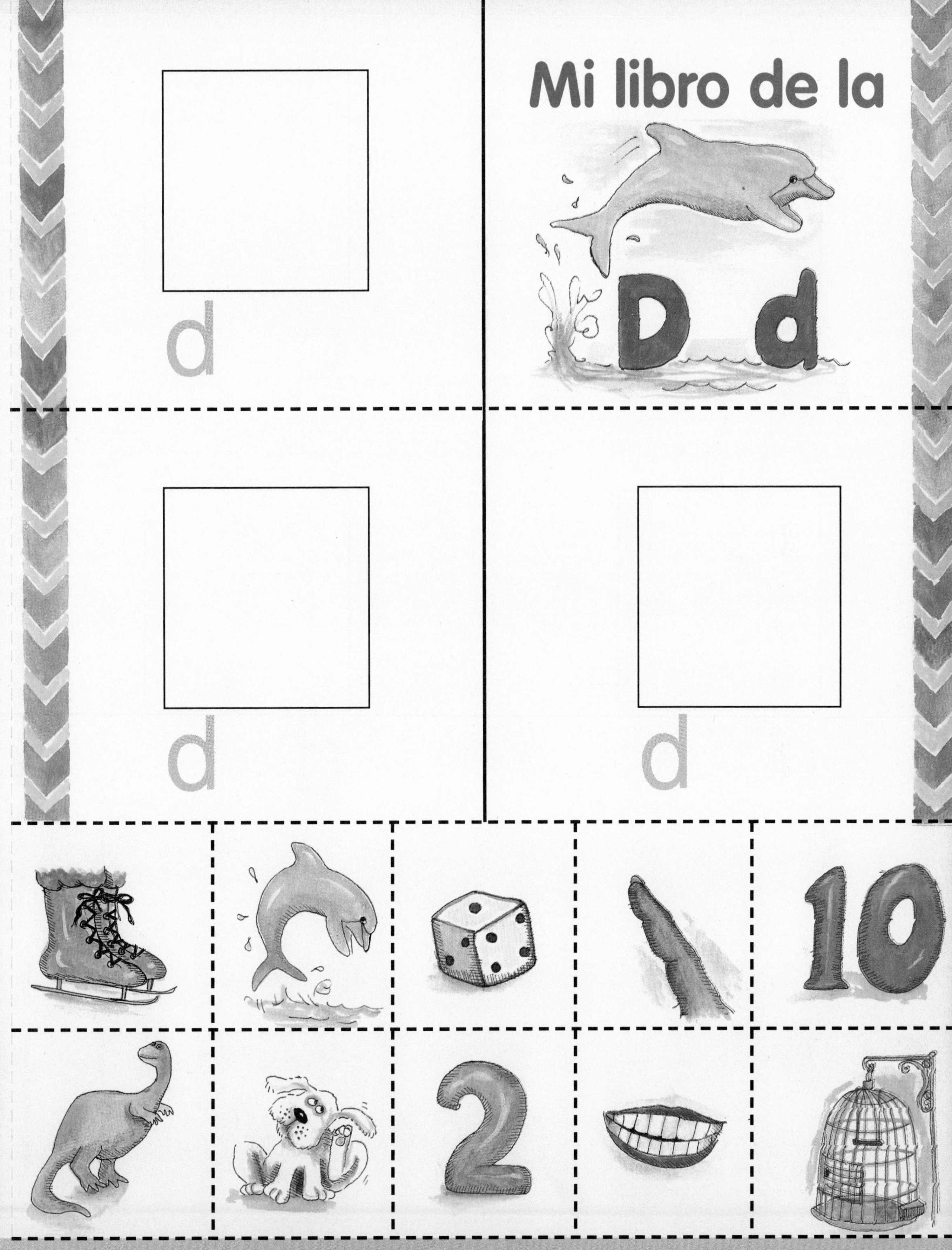

DIRECTIONS: Before children make this picture book, name the pictures: *patines, delfín, dado, dedo, diez, dinosaurio, perro, dos, dientes, jaula.* Ask children to paste a picture whose name begins with *d* on each page. They can then trace the *d* as they say the name of the object. Some children may also want to write the rest of the word.

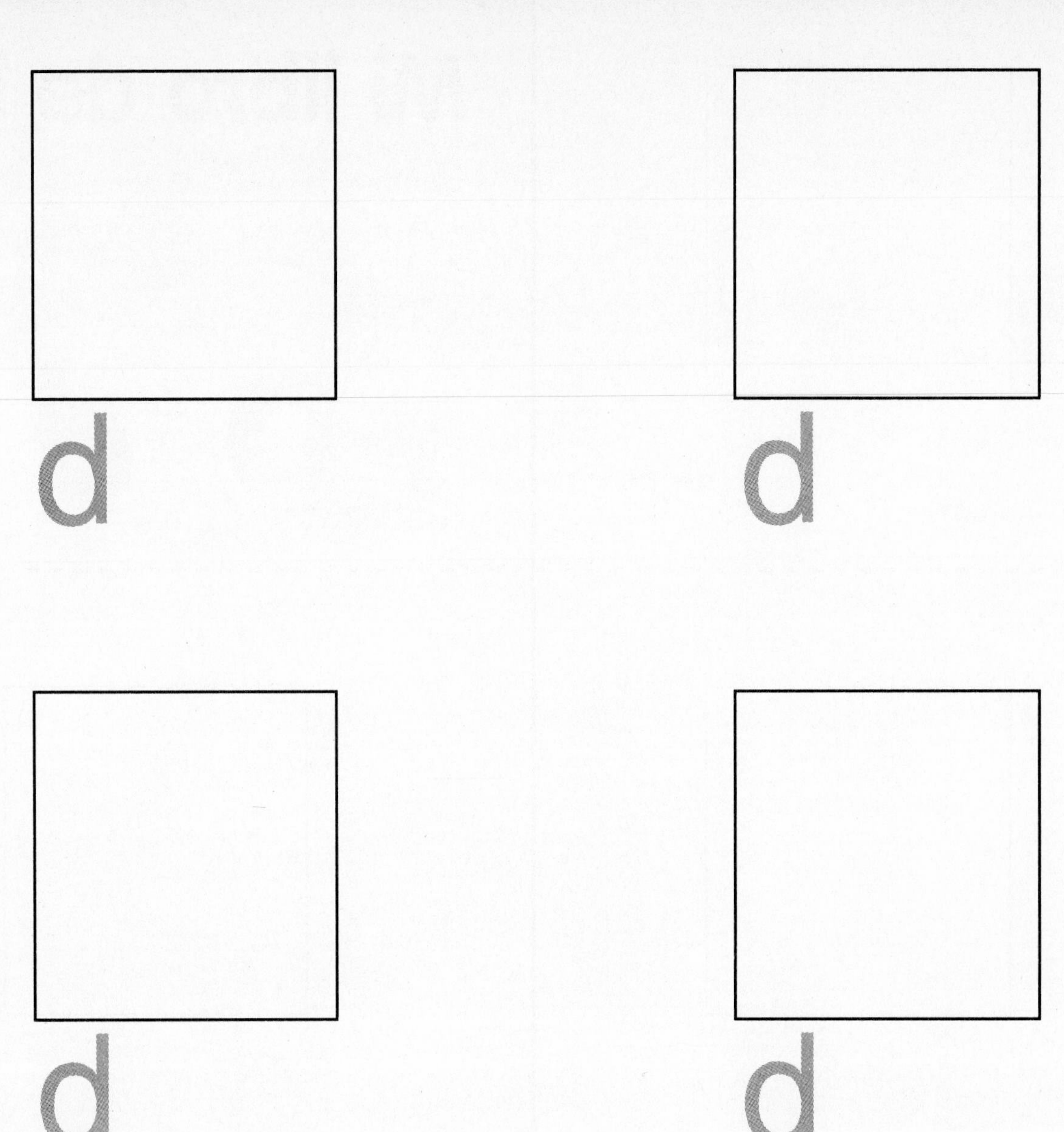
d
d
d
d

¿De quién es esta cola?

por ______________

______________ un pez.

3

______________ un pato.

5

DIRECTIONS: Children make a six-page picture book. Have them trace *Es de* on page 2 and write *Es de* on the line on the other pages to complete the sentence. Read the book with children as they track the print.

Es de una ballena.

2

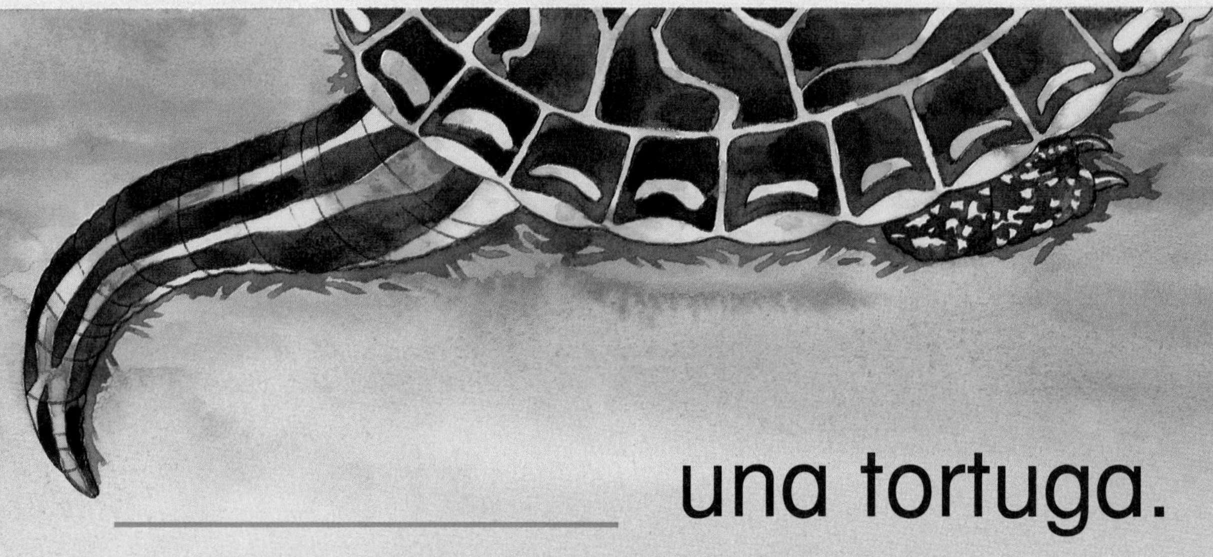

_____ una tortuga.

4

_____ un delfín.

6

C c conejo

Corre, corre lejos.

Escribe C c.

DIRECTIONS: Have children trace the *C-c*, identify the word that begins with *c* and circle the *c*. Then have them practice writing *c* in the box.

Querida familia:

Estamos estudiando la *c*. En el otro lado de esta hoja hay una rima sobre la *c*. Su hijo/a se la puede enseñar y pueden recitarla juntos.

En el siguiente cuadro, dibujen algunas cosas que empiecen con *c*, o peguen fotografías de esos objetos. Luego, completen la oración con el nombre de uno de ellos.

____________ empieza con c.

DIRECTIONS: Have children take this page home and work with their families to draw one or more objects whose names begin with *c*. Then, they complete the sentence with the name of one of them.

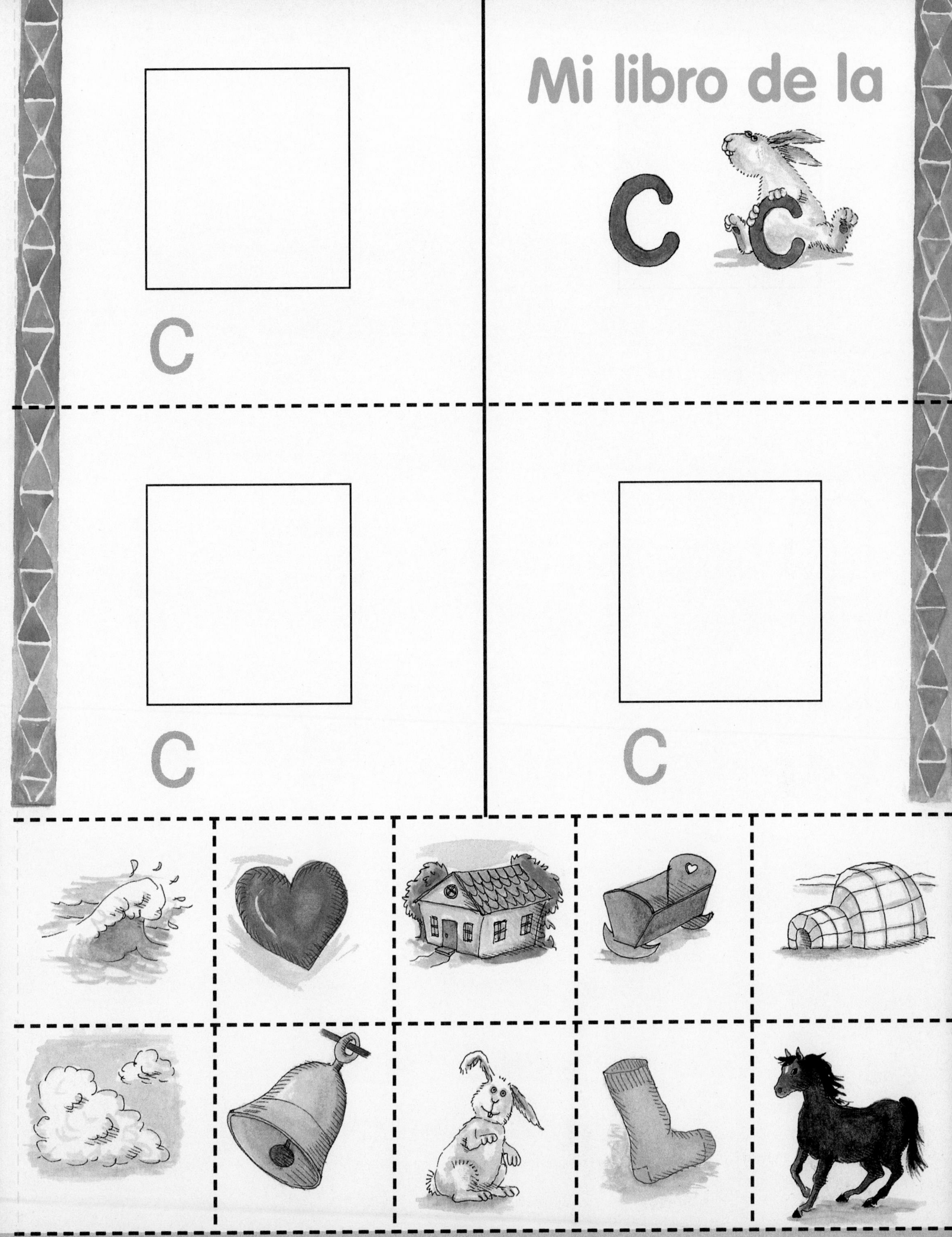

DIRECTIONS: Before children make this picture book, name the pictures: *ola, corazón, casa, cuna, iglú, nube, campaña, conejo, calcetín, caballo.* Ask children to paste a picture whose name begins with *c* on each page. They can then trace the *c* as they say the name of the object. Some children may also want to write the rest of the word.

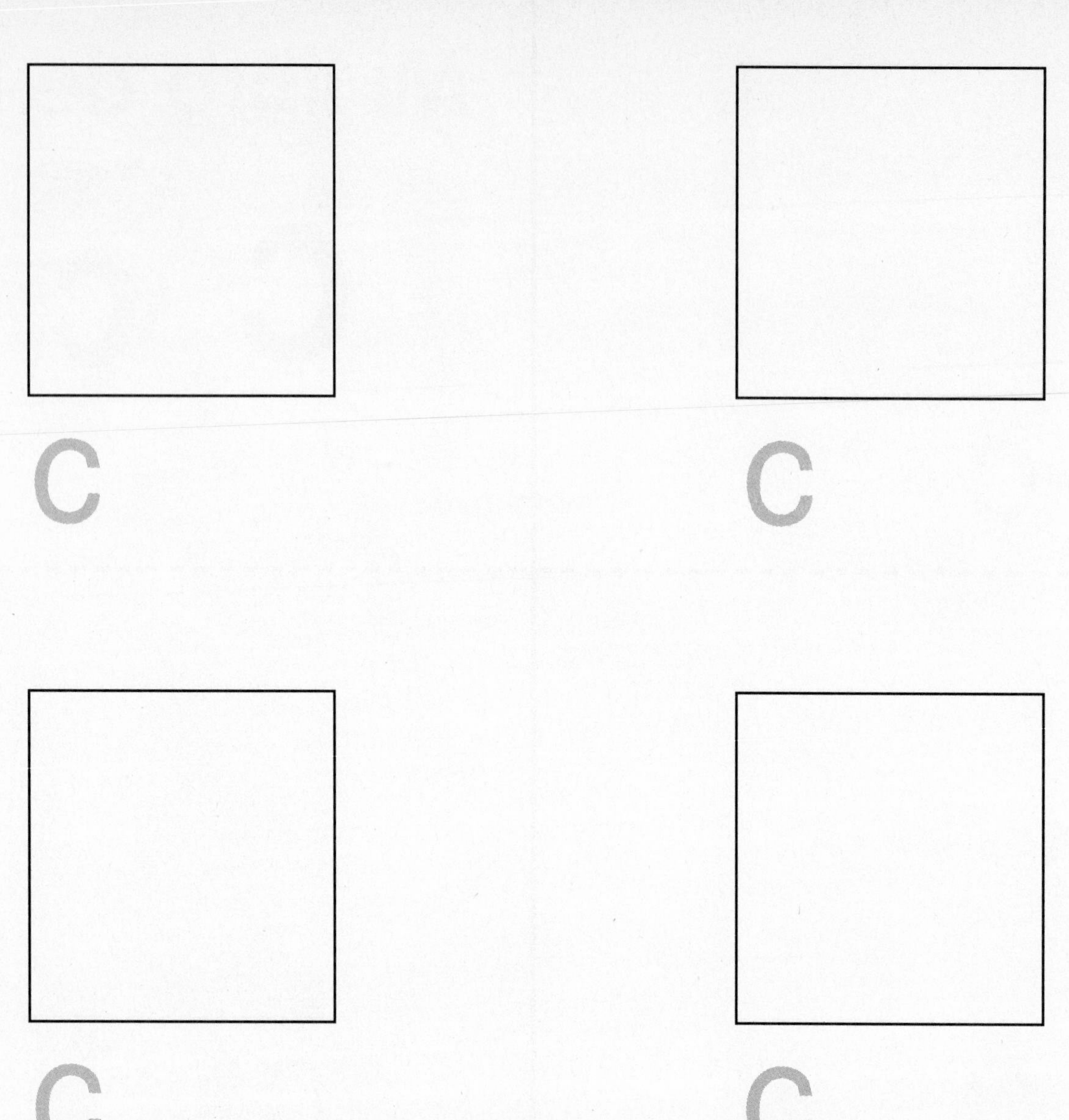
c
c
c
c

¡A comer!

por ____________

____________ fresas.

3

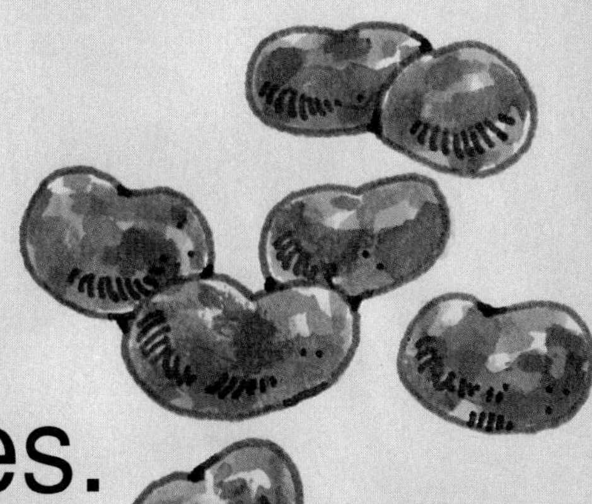

____________ frijoles.

5

DIRECTIONS: Children make a six-page picture book. Have them trace *Como* on page 2 and write *Como* on the line on the other pages to complete the sentence. Read the book with children as they track the print.

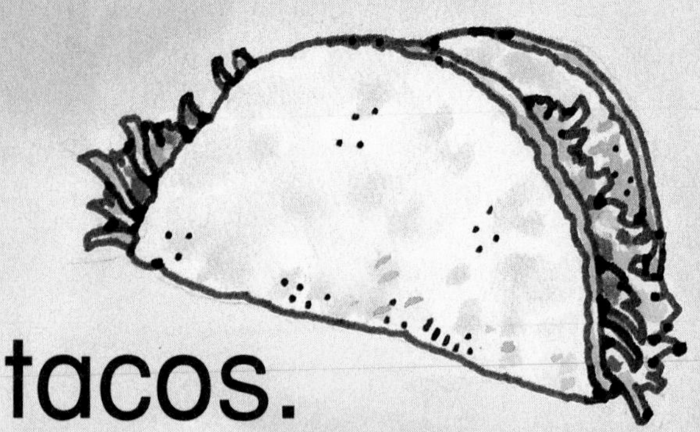

Como tacos.

2

_______ pollo.

4

_______ con mis amigos.

6

B b ballena

Tiene la panza llena.

Escribe B b.

DIRECTIONS: Have children trace the *B-b*, identify the word that begins with *b* and circle the *b*. Then have them practice writing *b* in the box.

Querida familia:

Estamos estudiando la *b*. En el otro lado de esta hoja hay una rima sobre la *b*. Su hijo/a se la puede enseñar y pueden recitarla juntos.

En el siguiente cuadro, dibujen algunas cosas que empiecen con *b*, o peguen fotografías de esos objetos. Luego, completen la oración con el nombre de uno de ellos.

____________ empieza con b.

DIRECTIONS: Have children take this page home and work with their families to draw one or more objects whose names begin with *b*. Then, they complete the sentence with the name of one of them.

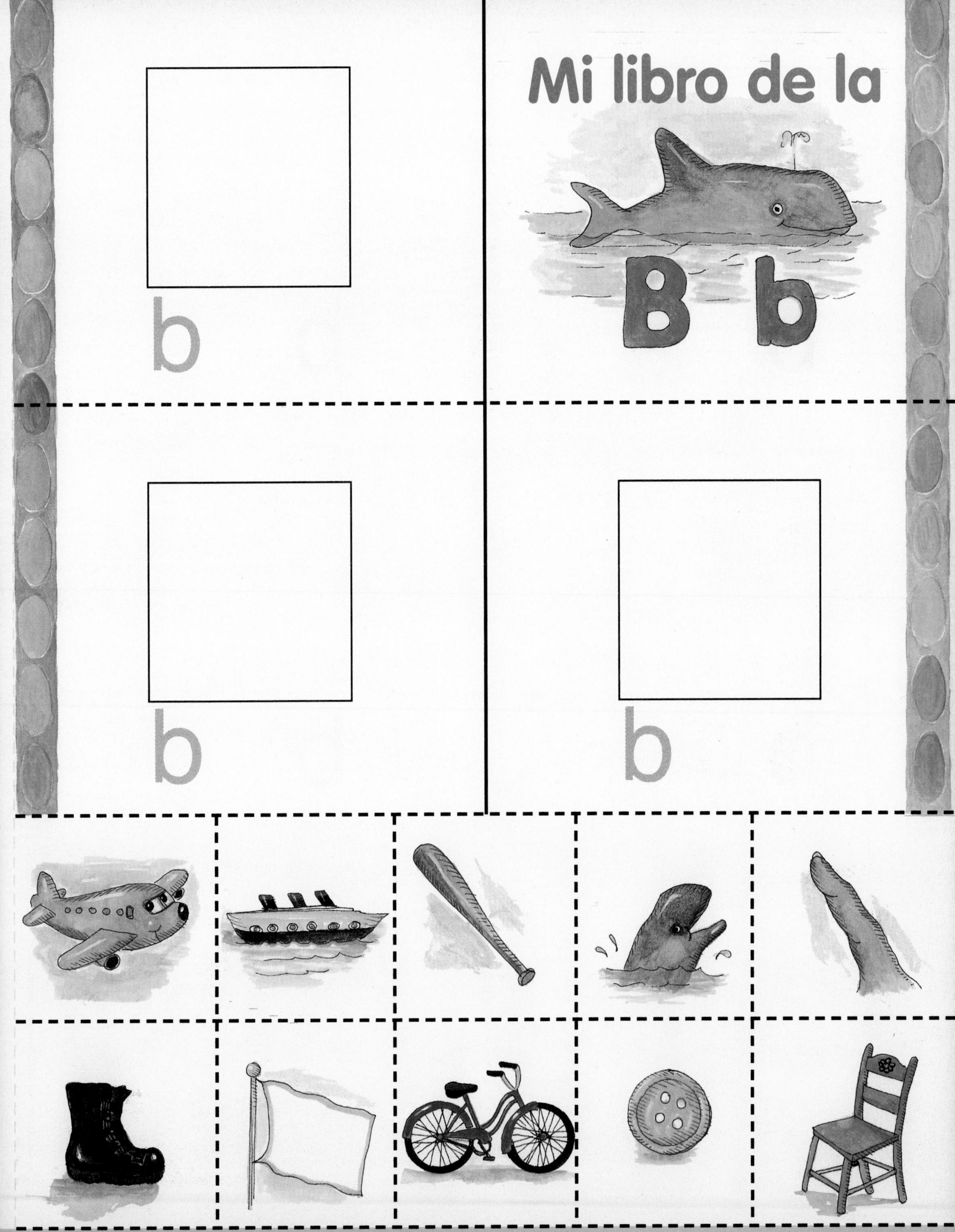

DIRECTIONS: Before children make this picture book, name the pictures: *avión, barco, bato, ballena, dedo, bota, bandera, bicicleta, botón, silla.* Ask children to paste a picture whose name begins with *b* on each page. They can then trace the *b* as they say the name of the object. Some children may also want to write the rest of the word.

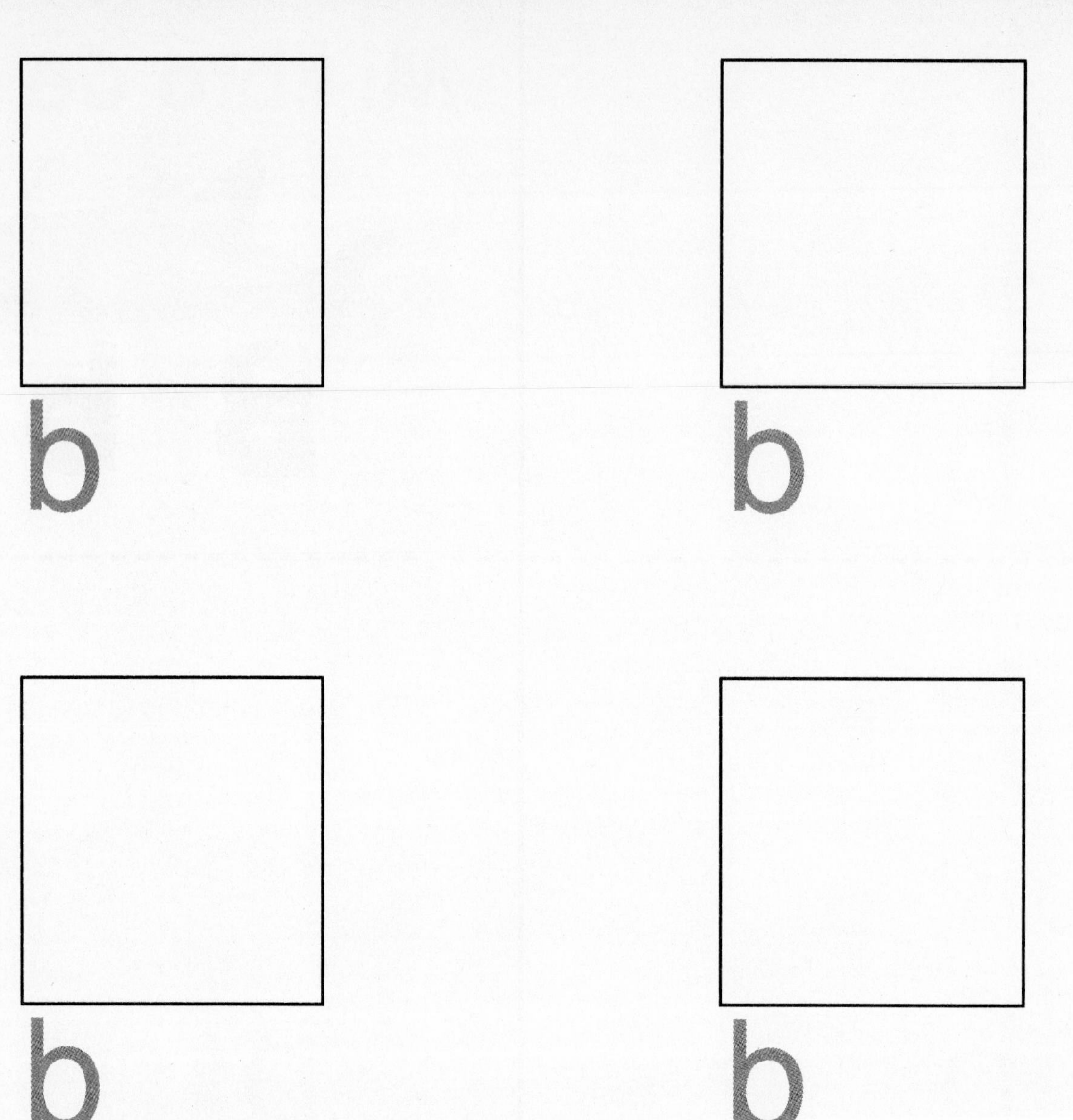
b
b
b
b

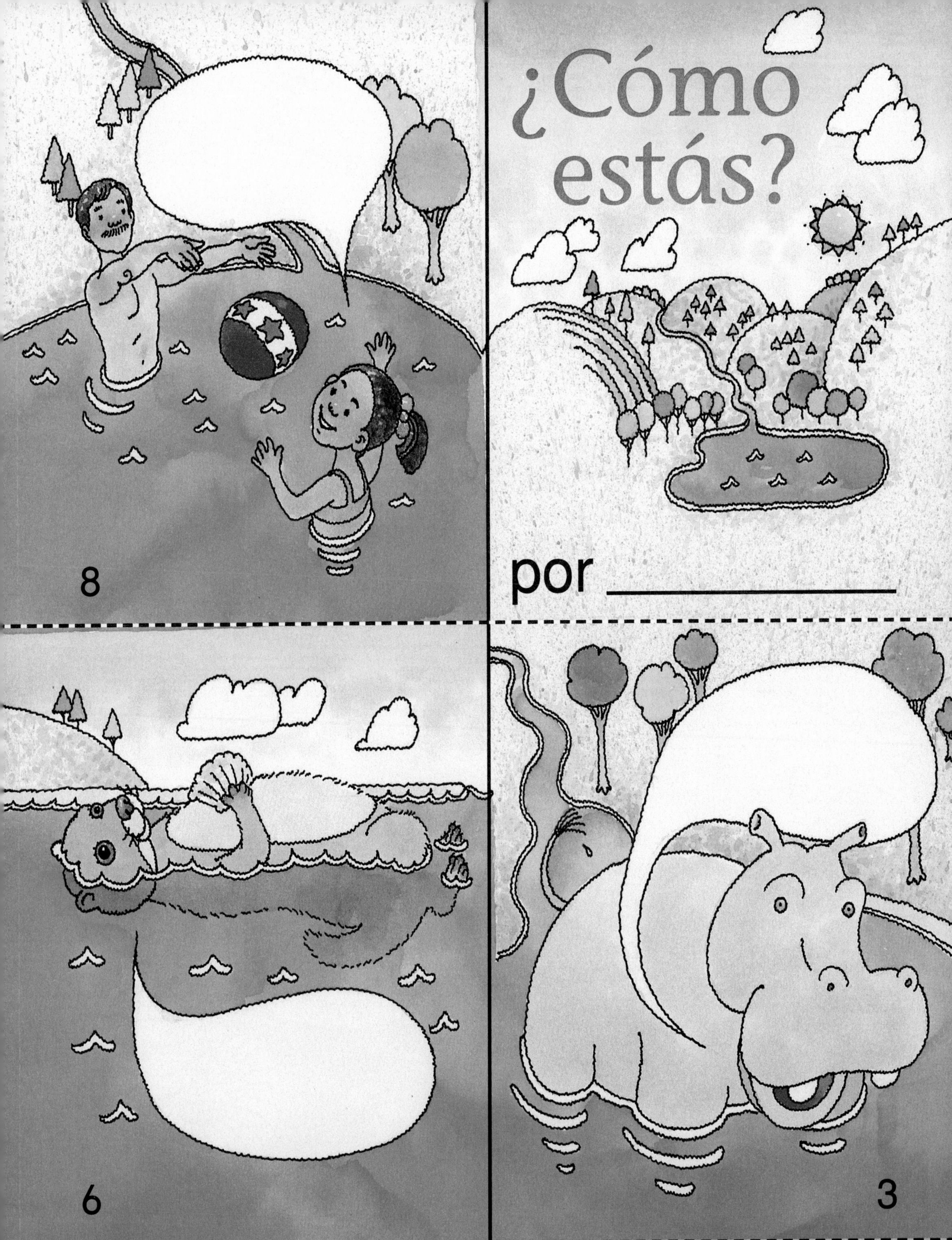

DIRECTIONS: Children make an eight-page picture book. Have them trace *bien* on page 2 and write *bien* in the speech balloons on pages 3–8.

bien
2
7
4
5

N n nutria

Tiene la cara sucia.

Escribe N n.

DIRECTIONS: Have children trace the *N-n*, identify the word that begins with *n* and circle the *n*. Then have them practice writing *n* in the box.

Querida familia:

Estamos estudiando la *n*. En el otro lado de esta hoja hay una rima sobre la *n*. Su hijo/a se la puede enseñar y pueden recitarla juntos.

En el siguiente cuadro, dibujen algunas cosas que empiecen con *n*, o peguen fotografías de esos objetos. Luego, completen la oración con el nombre de uno de ellos.

____________ empieza con n.

DIRECTIONS: Have children take this page home and work with their families to draw one or more objects whose names begin with *n*. Then, they complete the sentence with the name of one of them.

DIRECTIONS: Before children make this picture book, name the pictures: *nutria, nube, yate, sapo, nido, nariz, nueve, nuez, nudo, iguana*. Ask children to paste a picture whose name begins with *n* on each page. They can then trace the *n* as they say the name of the object. Some children may also want to write the rest of the word.

n

n

n

n

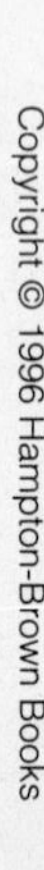

DIRECTIONS: Children make an eight-page picture book. Have them trace *no* on page 2 and write *no* under the pictures on pages 3–7. Read the book with children as they track the print.

no

2

7

4

5

R r rana

Se llama Juana.

Escribe R r.

DIRECTIONS: Have children trace the *R-r*, identify the word that begins with *r* and circle the *r*. Then have them practice writing *r* in the box.

Querida familia:

Estamos estudiando la *r*. En el otro lado de esta hoja hay una rima sobre la *r*. Su hijo/a se la puede enseñar y pueden recitarla juntos.

En el siguiente cuadro, dibujen algunas cosas que empiecen con *r*, o peguen fotografías de esos objetos. Luego, completen la oración con el nombre de uno de ellos.

________________ empieza con r.

DIRECTIONS: Have children take this page home and work with their families to draw one or more objects whose names begin with *r*. Then, they complete the sentence with the name of one of them.

DIRECTIONS: Before children make this picture book, name the pictures: *rosa, ratoncito, remo, estrella, ardilla, reloj, rueda, regla, pingüino, radio*. Ask children to paste a picture whose name begins with *r* on each page. They can then trace the *r* as they say the name of the object. Some children may also want to write the rest of the word.

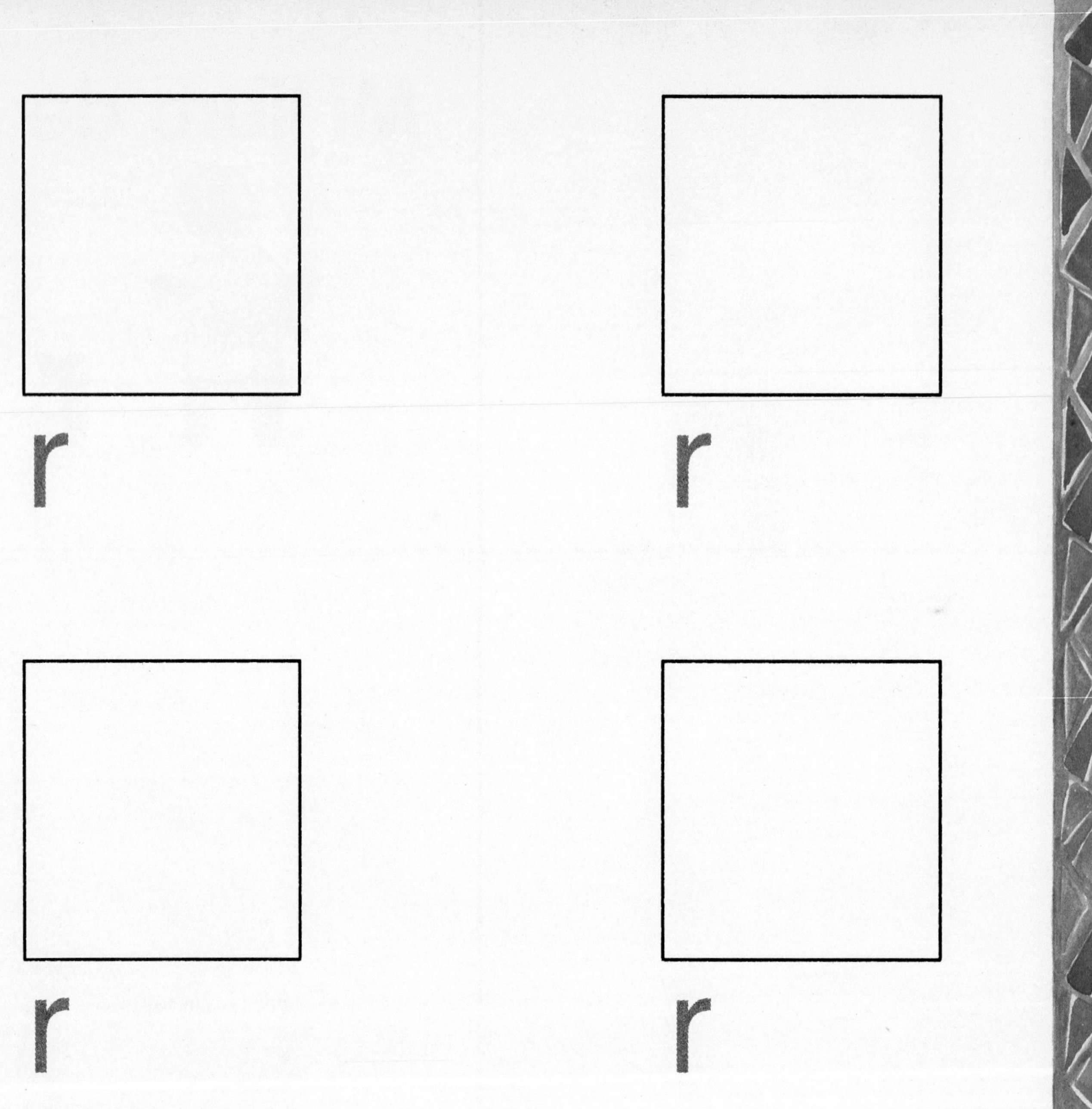
r
r
r
r

8

por ___________

todo ______

6

árbol ______

3

DIRECTIONS: Children make an eight-page picture book. Have them trace *rojo* on page 2 and write *rojo* on the line on pages 3, 4, 5, and 6. Read the book with children as they track the print.

sol rojo

2

7

pasto ______ pájaro ______

4

5